PRINCIPLES OF PUBLISHING
In
The Digital Age
5th Edition

Theresa M. Moore

www.antellus.com

Principles of Publishing In The Digital Age – 5th Edition

Copyright 2019 Theresa M. Moore, all rights reserved.

Interior illustrations by Theresa M. Moore copyright © 2018, 2019
Published by **Antellus**, Los Angeles, California **www.antellus.com**
Catalog no. 022 ISBN 978-1-7325312-8-4

Other nonfiction books by Theresa M. Moore:

♦ A BOOK OF FIVE RINGS: A Practical Guide to Strategy by Miyamoto Musashi; *A Modern Translation For the 21st Century by Theresa M. Moore*
♦ The Most Important Science Fiction Films of The 20th Century Vols 1-3
♦ Science Fiction Films of The 20th Century: The Early Years
♦ Science Fiction Films of The 20th Century: The 1940s
♦ Science Fiction Films of The 20th Century: 1950-1954
♦ Science Fiction Films of The 20th Century: 1955-1956
♦ Science Fiction Films of The 20th Century: 1957
♦ Science Fiction Films of The 20th Century: 1958

TABLE OF CONTENTS

INTRODUCTION

I wrote the first edition in response to much of the chatter I read in numerous internet forums, where it seemed that there was no end to the number of newbies posting queries about this or that aspect of publishing. Some of the threads overlapped. These people seemed to have no clue even how to write a book and were begging for help. Others expressed the same questions about how to do this or that to publish, from formatting their books to bypassing difficulties with other situations, from marketing to dealing with internet etiquette to engaging in contract affiliations with other publishers. After reading the same lamentations for the thousandth time I decided that it was time to share my own learning experiences in the world of publishing.

I was not new to publishing in the old print process, having participated in writing and illustrating stories for small press publications and fanzines. I was already a writer and artist when I was introduced to mimeographic and dittographic printing. I still love the smell of ditto ink; it reminds me of when we got our notes and tests in school and we used to sniff the freshly printed paper. It smelled so… scholastic. But I digress.

In college I took courses in layout and advertising design. By the time I graduated I knew how to prepare a professional looking flyer, brochure, or whatever was needed on paper. While I was there I prepared flyers announcing events for various campus groups. I learned about transfer lettering and dot screen film (thank the gods for Zipatone™!), ruling lines and spacing, layout and paste up.

I worked inhouse at several printing companies and publishers that shipped out their art to be processed after the paste up of each page was made. The smell of rubber cement also comes to mind. It used to give me headaches. I learned how to cut rubylith, to mask the negative images, and how to use various typesetting machines to produce copy and headlines. I learned the advantages and the limitations of those processes. Other houses worked in 4-color serigraphic printing and rotogravure, but those processes were expensive for me to use on my own projects so I was forced to stick to black ink applications at the time.

I also worked for a screen printing company and learned how the screens were made, what kind of inks were used and how to clean them. At the time the company only worked the old fashioned way, by providing a screen for each color of ink used. But my job did not last long as I also got headaches from the fumes of ink and cleaners, and my doctor advised me to quit.

At the time the quality and types of small press magazines and fanzines varied. Some consisted of pages of dittoed or mimeographed "newsletters", assembled and then stapled together to share among the contributors. We called these "zines", which became the output of APAs, short for Amateur Press Associations. They were actually the forerunners of what we now call "internt forums", and their articles were "blogs" in print. They consisted of commentary about this or that genre or subject, an observation, or a review of a book or movie. Others gradually developed into anthologies of short stories written by fans of this or that genre, some illustrated and assembled into large volumes of fiction, and sold only for the cost to print.

This is not what we call "fan fiction". These were original stories or articles written whole cloth from the writers' own imaginations; while fan fiction were original stories written by fans about characters from specific films or television shows. I published two fanzine series of my own during that time, but not having access to an economical binding service I was forced to staple the pages together, then slip a plastic report spine over the edges to make it stable. Each series died out as interest in the specific subject waned, and there was no longevity to their collectible value.

While there is a great deal of controversy about fan fiction from the view of the various television and film producers, which see these imaginative offspring as a violation of copyright and intellectual property appropriation, fan fiction does and continues to persist to this day. That no one makes any real money from these ventures makes no difference. It is the love of the particular subject which propogates the stories, and their writers have done their homework.

Nevertheless, any *serious* author must acknowledge that there is a vast difference between fan fiction and that which most traditional publishers view as original and created entirely by the author from his own imagination. To that end, the publishers do not accept fan fiction for publication and there is a true and legal danger of liability for copyright infringement.

Lately, the standards have relaxed somewhat when books like "Fifty Shades of Grey" were published, which originated from fan fiction with the names and place changed to avoid ingringement.

When photocopy processing was developed I embraced it as the up and coming thing. But here there were several limitations as well. Pages processed by thermal imaging had a tendency to fade over time, and the paper was too delicate and easy to destroy. As companies like Xerox® and Canon® kept tinkering with the process, they improved the quality of reproduction and made it easier to copy documents by developing the photocopy process.

Then one day along came *color* photocopy. The quality was not up to maximum then, and the colors had a tendency to fade or change color, sometimes with applications of waxy inks. At that time I belonged to a fan club that published their own monthly newsletter and I helped them to prepare their galleys, sometimes creating full color covers for them. I learned what limitations there were in that medium, too.

While I was thus occupied I wanted to do still more, and to streamline the process to make my own writing available to the wider public. But I was not sure which direction to go and there were very few resources. Companies like Microsoft® and Apple® were working on improving and expanding the storage capacity of their computers, but many people did not own their own desktop computers yet. Google and Yahoo did not yet exist. Netscape was a burbling infant crawling on the floor. BlackBerry and full feature cell phones were a twinkle in someone's eye, inspired by science fiction and fantasy films.

As I watched all this activity I know that one day the publishing industry would experience a revolution. As personal computers became the powerhouse tools they are today, so did the development of software to enable one to publish a complete book in a variety of sizes and formats.

Then, in 2003, along came *print on demand*. Okay, I said it. POD. **PRINT ON DEMAND.**

In 2005, while I was looking on the internet for an economical way to get just one book printed, I discovered *Lulu.com*. Lulu was the most prolific printer of POD books, art, photo albums and other printed products for the time. I looked at the site, studied the FAQ (Frequently Asked Questions), and quickly learned that I could have a book published without spending anything in advance.

Later I discovered that dealing with Lulu was frought with obstacles. Lulu had a black mark against it for not offering a return policy on books ordered through them. No professional bookseller would deal with them, and the authors who signed on to have their books printed and distributed have been met with delays in listings, distribution issues and a slowdown in payouts, all of which have resulted in Lulu's downward spiral into some obscurity.

Soon afterward Lulu added on a series of "distribution channels" which included access to Amazon.com's vast bookselling channel, and/or access to booksellers like Barnes & Noble, Borders, Waterstones and Blackwell. But this cost more money than it was worth, since along with the fee for distribution the retail price of any book soared into the stratosphere.

There is already a stigma attached to the process itself due to propaganda circulated by supporters of the "traditional" publishers, who view this as a competitive end run around their profit margins. They do not want you to know about POD. They look down their collective noses at the independent publisher because they were looking at the future and they were afraid of it. In their world, many really good writers are ignored, or rejected by agents who are swamped by submissions and like it that way because it reduces the competition. The "gateway" position they placed themselves in also increased the number of really good books which will never see print. So much for freedom of the press. There is also no guarantee that the books themselves were really that good.

True, many books put out in the POD format are down to outright **B.A.D.**, as there is no quality control for the authors or their work. But the reader's interest determines the success or failure of any author, so there is no danger that we will be flooded with stinkers; and one either sinks or swims in this business. The bottom line is that the stinkers will go unsold, while the stars will emerge to shine. POD is not the problem. It is a process; a tool like any other. To fault the process is to miss the point.

With print on demand, there is no inventory to keep on hand, no cost except the cost of printing and shipping and a commission paid on the sale price once the book is sold. You can be published in a matter of minutes if you prepare your project right. There is no guarantee that you will become famous this way, but you will be successful as long as you are loyal to your own project. If you have a story to tell, you now have a chance to make it available to readers at a relatively low cost and you also have the option to sell them yourself in whatever manner you choose.

The advent of the *ebook* (or e-book) has also created a diverse marketplace, as the world begins to find ways to get around the deforestation of the planet by going paperless. Of course, even storage becomes an iffy proposition in a world dependent on electricity to make things work, because there is no guarantee that these devices and products will last forever. But for those who cannot afford to haul a library of books and papers around with them wherever they go, the ebook has proved its worth.

As the technology to make reading ebooks develops and improves, the prevalence of the ereader as a mobile device will make its importance more critical to those seeking to get their books out there in front of their target consumers: people who have purchased ereaders so that they can take their library with them wherever they go. The ebook was developed for ease of use and convenience. It is merely a matter of using the software properly in order to produce economical files which can be stored on these devices. I have devoted a special section to digital books, devices and also that strange new rights clause: DRM, which everyone keeps talking about, but never likes. DRM is basically a lock against copyright infringement, but which already been hacked into several times and has proven to be a hindrance, not a help.

Take heart that the printed book is not likely to be replaced anytime soon. The value of a book on paper is appreciated by those who know that, should the world lose its ability to use electrical power, the hard copy of the human record will still be there in a relatively permanent form, as it has been for centuries.

This, too is an ephemeral concept since paper itself is subject to the ravages of age, damage, and fire. The records of the ancients were kept on more durable materials like iron, bronze, precious metals and stone, but most were not portable. India began keeping records on palm leaves bound in sheaves, and they retain their freshness to this day.

If you are in search of a self-help publisher there is a dozen of them out there, hoping that you will plunk down cash to have them print your books. On any given day I receive a postcard from a subsidy publisher or a large volume printing firm extolling their services for *only* $1,000 per title, and that is just the set up charge. Printing each book costs more. Some of these services demand a minimum print run per title. Publicity and promotion cost still more. The cumulative effect of these charges is that you can easily spend more than $2,000 or more before you see a single copy roll off the printer.

Today I have published 25 books and an equal number of ebooks; several of which have gone out of print. They are sold all over the world online. I achieved this success by feeling my way around and making mistakes just like the rest of you. But I succeeded at producing books that are just as good in quality as those of the big house publishers. All it takes is dedication and the will to learn, and you too can be a successful author or publisher in a matter of a few days.

In this book I will show you what I learned to do so you can start yourself on your way. Here you will find a vast quantity of resources that will help you publish and promote your project. I will also discuss copyright law and registration of your book, as well as accounting, legal and taxation issues you need to pay attention to ensure your continued success; as well as the pitfalls you may encounter.

This information is offered for the publication of a book, but it can be applied to any product you want to sell, whether it is a music file, a video, a toy, or other sundry item. What you do with the knowledge is entirely up to you.

--*Theresa M. Moore*

The History of Books and Printing

Before we begin with the basics I want to acquaint you with a brief history of the publishing industry, which has had a long and glorious run from neolithic times to today.

In The Beginning The first books were scrolls of demotic script written by scribes employed by the pharoahs of Egypt as long ago as 4,000 BC, and are the earliest known records kept on a material other than stone. Before that, many of the earliest records and books were carved into wax and stone by the ancient Sumerians, in what is modern Iraq. The first ancient laws *on the books* were written there and were used to spread a system of law across the known world.

An example of Egyptian demotic script on papyrus, a paper made of reed leaves which were pressed together.

An example of Sumerian cuneiform script. This was often created with wood tools on clay, which was then air dried and then fired to hardness.

As the Egyptians and Greeks conquered more and more territory, they brought writing to the early dynasties of Mongols, who in turn gave rise to China. Soon after that, the Chinese developed their own system of writing and record keeping, and are famous for keeping the earliest known astronomical almanacs and horoscopes in the world.

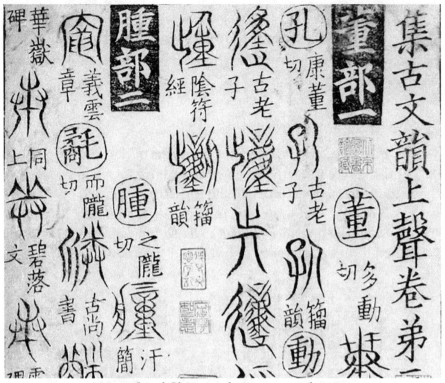
A sample of Chinese characters and script.

As successive dynasties were born, and the Greeks and Romans began to flourish and broaden their empires, writing and books became necessary to maintain an educated nobility and bureaucracy. Greek slaves knowing how to read and write enjoyed the same privileges as Roman nobles.

While this was going on, successive Persian and Chinese conquerors made good use of these skills. There was no common language yet, so letters exchanged among the kings and emperors were translated. The translations were written down by the scribes to keep a record of what was said and bound into books. Tibetan priests kept records of the history of their region on folded sheets of parchment or palm leaves, bound between two boards and tied with silk.

There was no formal system of education then, so the only people who could read or write were from the upper classes. The peasants were allowed a cursory oral education from the temple priests, who selected only a few to become scribes.

Around 200 AD the Chinese developed the wood block printing method, a technique for printing text, images or patterns on textiles and later paper. The wood block method was to pass ink over a carved plate of wood, then lay down a sheet of rice paper and allow it to absorb the ink. The result speeded up the process of copying. The earliest surviving examples from China date to before 220 BC, and from Egypt to the 4th century AD.

A sample of Chinese woodblock printing.

The Middle Ages - When the Roman empire fell in the 4th century AD, there followed a period of "darkness", that is: we don't really know how many books were written or kept during this time. In 415 the archbishop Cyril declared many books of the world to be evil and ordered the Library of Alexandria to be burned, and in the conflagration thousands of scrolls and valuable books kept there were destroyed. It is rumored that many of these scrolls found their way into the hands of men who had more secular views, and who were able to escape into the hinterlands to preserve as much as they could. But I guess we will never know the truth about that.

From the 7th to 13th century AD, the age of religious "manuscript" book production began. Books in this period are entirely constructed by hand, and were largely religious texts whose creation was meant as an act of worship. Christian monks occupied themselves with creating beautifully illuminated manuscripts and copied what was then a

3

coptic bible for distribution to priests, abbots, kings and their courts. These books were reserved only for the nobles and bureaucracy because the peasants were not considered worthy of receiving a formal education.

Notable among these books are *The Book of Kells*, and *The Book of Durrow*, which were hand inscribed and illustrated from scratch each time. One could not really call them copies. Each of these books was meticulously hand lettered and painted, then heavily embellished with thin sheets of gold leaf. And by gold I mean 24 karat, not the cheap stuff in use today. The miniature versions you see now are but pale shadows of the massive volumes which were the originals. There are other books of this type in existence, but many have fallen into disrepair or been destroyed by age, war, and neglect.

There was also little incentive to distribute the books to the general public due to the lack of access to the monastic libraries. Given the amount of time and energy and financial resources that went into their production, books were far too valuable, so there was no way to use them for scholarship. This problem was compounded by the lack of a uniform cataloging system in the monasteries. Even if one did have access, there was no no way of knowing what was in the collection, or where it might be located. And as most monasteries were insular and preoccupied with self-examination before God, they were unwilling to open up their doors and allow free access to laymen.

A page from the Book of Kells

An example from the Book of Durrow

Screen printing first appeared in a recognizable form in China during the Song Dynasty (960–1279 AD). Japan and other Asian countries adopted this method of printing and advanced the craft by using it in conjunction with block printing and hand applied paints. Screen printing was introduced to Western Europe sometime in the late 18th century, but did not gain large acceptance or use in Europe until silk mesh was more available for trade from the east. Screen printing was first patented in England by Samuel Simon in 1907.

An example of Chinese screen printing on silk

The world's first known movable type system for printing was created in China around 1040 AD by Bi Sheng (990–1051 AD) during the Song Dynasty. Then the first metal movable type system for printing was made in Korea during the Goryeo Dynasty (around 1230 AD). This led to the printing of the Jikji in 137; today the oldest known movable type print book. The diffusion of both movable type systems were limited They were expensive and required an enormous amount of time and labor to manipulate the thousands of ceramic tablets in use, or in the case of Korea, metal tablets.

Notice I have not even mentioned Gütenberg yet.

From the 13th to 15th centuries there came a secularization of book production. Books were produced that did not serve as aids for worship but which tried to explain the natural world. The difficulty was that production was still taking place via manuscript creation methods. The production of secular books was driven by two things: the rise of universities in Europe as centers of inquiry, spreading from Italy and Rome; and the return of the crusaders from Jerusalem in the 13th century, who brought with them books from Byzantium. These books, written during the Greek and Roman periods in history, focused on real-world concerns and contained works of science, some of which challenged the edicts of the church; but I digress.

Along with these developments, Marco Polo returned from the far East with the knowledge of printing and book making, whom he passed to his sons, along with a colorful tale of the Chinese civilization at full flower. It was soon after his arrival in Italy that the plague began to interrupt the course of European civilization, and he died before many of the inventions he found there were developed. The chief contribution of the Polo household was spaghetti, which was based on the Chinese noodle, and gunpowder. Beyond that, science and astronomy foundered because they flew in the face of church edict.

While the Indians were composing their *Upanishads*, the *Mahabarat*, and the *Baghavaad Gita*, Middle Eastern scholars celebrated poetry, mathematics, and the written word of Mohammed in their own books. The number of texts which began to circulate throughout the known world was staggering. Yet only the courtly privileged and well educated officers of the church had access to the vast wealth of knowledge and science.

When the virulence of the plague finally dissipated in the 15th century, the first printed books began to appear. Among these were traditional works like the Bible, books of hours (prayer books) and the religious calendars. Books composed of wood block prints were popular, and "cartoon" art began to appear. The shift in consciousness that occurred with this period of history gave rise to the notion that reality could be accurately represented. Science started to be popular because it was different.

The technology of the printing press, coupled with the surrounding changes in the political/economic system, changed the way Western Europe saw its place in the world. This period saw the advent and expansion of a European-dominated world economy and the beginning of a system of international competition for trade among independent states.

The Renaissance - Things begin to change when, in 1452, Johannes Gütenberg conceived of the idea for a printing press. He brought together the technologies of paper, oil-based ink and the wine press to print books on block print plates, then later with movable type. The printing press was not a single invention. It was the aggregation of several technologies in one place. That cell phone you are holding is an aggregation of technologies. Every element was invented separately and then brought together to create the whole. Innovation is a marvelous development.

One thing to remember is that Gütenberg gets credit for an invention thought to have been developed simultaneously in Holland and in Prague, a city in Poland.

Gütenberg championed mass production paper making techniques. Paper was brought from China to Italy in the 13th century, but was thought to be too flimsy for books. Before then, books were made of vellum (calf or lamb skin) because of its durability. However, vellum was too costly to produce for printed books. So he employed the use of parchment instead.

He also worked to develop oil based inks. These had been around since the 10th century, but smeared on the vellum used to make books. The religious manuscripts were painted with an egg based tempera composed of ground minerals and precious stones. This was unsuitable for printing with type because the tempera broke down too easily and had a tendency to fade with time.

Gütenberg's other contribution to printing was the development of a punch and mold system which allowed for mass production of the movable type used to reproduce a page of text. These letters would be put together in a type tray which was then used to print a page of text. If a letter broke down, it could be easily replaced. When the printing of copies of one page was finished, the type could be cleaned and then reused for the next page or the next book.

One of several pictures of Johannes Gütenberg. I happen to think that this is the right one because it was printed using a Gütenberg press.

The first books to show up in print shops were bibles and religious tracts, the most famous of which is the **King James Bible**, the basic text of the combination of the Old and New Testaments into one, which was carefully vetted and edited by the church to remove any "dangerous" ideas. The history of that particular book would fill a book all by itself, so we will not dwell on it here. But it was the first time a bible was translated into a language other than Latin, as Latin was the language of the church. There were also the books of Psalms and Hymns, religious pamphlets about particular books of the bible, and so on.

The Gütenberg press, showing its basic scale and size. It could be adapted for any size page or text.

The next books to attract publishers were the "humanist" texts brought back from Byzantium by Crusaders, and other texts of antiquity; but there was little or no printing of new ideas. The printing business at that time was in constant flux. The distribution of books was poorly organized. The market was there, and the potential for filling the demand, but the transport, control and "advertising" mechanisms were not in place.

In addition, there was still a low literacy rate in Europe. Most people did not know how to read at all, much less in Latin. But illiterate people still had access to books because of traveling entertainers, who stood in the marketplace and read from books to earn a living. Crowds gathered in the town square to listen and learn, even if none of them owned a book.

The thirst for knowledge was keen and the people felt they had more control over their own lives as long as they knew what was going on in the world around them. Remember that in those days people rarely traveled, and some lived and died in the same village where they were born.

The situation was improved by the introduction of the Frankfort Book Faire, which exists to this day. Cities in Europe held fairs the way they do today, featuring whatever the surrounding area produced.

Frankfort was the center for printing and so its fair drew publishers, booksellers, collectors, and scholars, who could participate and help to coordinate supply and demand, and by doing so earn a marginal living selling books. The fair also produced a catalog of all the works shown - an early Books in Print.

Yet book printing did not pose much of a challenge to the power and prestige of the church. Early print books were still conservative in content, and were filled with medieval images and ideas. Albrecht Dürer tried to turn the print medium into a serious space for art. He worked out a visual language that could show the intricate details of a scene. While he used a kind of Renaissance perspective in the construction of his images, he was also interested in anatomy and detail, all the while maintaining a medieval quality to the content of the drawing. Many of his drawings were allegorical, so that less educated readers could get the intent of the text all in one go.

During this time, in addition to Bibles and prayer books, there was traditional material in print: romances such as Giovanni Boccaccio's *De Claris Mulieribus* (Concerning Famous Women.), the pamphlets of Copernicus, Gallileo Galilei and other scientists, simple romances and adventures; as well as the premier of Chaucer's *Canterbury Tales*.

The printed book quickly became a popular possession in the world, so that by 1501 there were at least a thousand printing shops in Europe, which had produced 35,000 titles and 20 million copies.

At the same time, printing took off in other forms. Etching was brought into use by Daniel Hopfer (1470–1536), who is believed to have been the first to apply the technique to printmaking. Etching is the process of using strong acid or mordant to cut into the unprotected parts of a metal surface to create a design, called *intaglio*. In modern manufacturing other chemicals are used on other types of material in the same manner. As a method of printmaking it is, along with engraving, the most important technique for old master prints, and remains widely used today.

Another method was *mezzotint*, technically a drypoint method. It was the first tonal method to be used, enabling halftones to be produced without using line or dot based techniques like hatching, crosshatching or stipple. One roughens the plate with thousands of little dots made by a metal tool with small teeth, called a "rocker". In printing, the tiny pits in the plate hold the ink when the face of the plate is wiped clean. A high level of quality and richness in the print can be achieved. This method is also in use today, but only among artists and fine print makers.

The Reformation - The real innovation in culture, as related to print, is in the Protestant Reformation. Martin Luther's ideas took wing in the early to mid-1500s in Germany. In 1536, John Calvin published his work in Strasbourg, then moved to Geneva, Switzerland to escape the persecution of the church. The Reformation was the first revolutionary mass movement, in part because it took full advantage of the power of printed propaganda.

Much of this propaganda took form in images. One popular target for such images was the pope, as portrayed by Lucas Cranach in *The Whore of Babylon*. But the major producer of images at the time was still Dürer, whose "Vision of Seven Candlesticks", where Christ appears to John was popular fare.

In another series of what might be termed "political cartoons" entitled *The Passion of Christ and Anti-Christ,* Luther contrasted the life and actions of Christ with those of the Pope. This kind of propaganda was effective in challenging the power of the Roman Catholic church, primarily because the church itself had done a terrible job of educating the otherwise illiterate masses so far. While few book audiences of today would know the story of *The Whore of Babylon*, virtually all of Europe was familiar with the text and was capable of understanding what the cartoon meant. They weren't blind or stupid; they simply did not know how to read.

Of course, this whole campaign blew up in the Protestants' faces, as the King of France and his allies drove them out of Europe under pressure from the church. This in turn caused them to make the perilous journey across the ocean to the New World. And church edicts to crack down on anti-Catholic thought made heretics and witches out of scientists and philosophers. Truly, the advent of the book changed the world significantly during this time and it looked like the Renaissance was going to fizzle and go out.

Around 1642 *aquatint* appeared. Aquatint is an intaglio printmaking technique, a variant of etching. A copper or zinc plate is etched with acid. The inked plate is passed through a printing press together with a sheet of paper, resulting in a transfer of the ink to the paper. This can be repeated a number of times depending on the particular technique employed. Aquatint also made it possible to print in color, though that was a more labor-intensive process. Each color required a separate plate, and the etching must be precise or the colors would muddy or print "off register". It enabled more copies of an illustration or print to be made at one time, but still made the whole book expensive to produce.

The Age of Reason - We cannot ignore the foresight of Benjamin Franklin (January 17, 1706-April 17, 1790) when he brought the printing press to New England in 1726. Franklin was one of the founding fathers of the United States of America. A noted polymath, Franklin was a leading author and printer, politician, postmaster, scientist, inventor, satirist, civic activist, statesman, and diplomat. As a scientist, he was a major figure in the American Enlightenment and the history of physics for his discoveries and theories regarding electricity. He invented the lightning rod, bifocals, the Franklin stove, a carriage odometer, and the glass 'armonica'. He formed both the first public lending library in America and the first fire department in Pennsylvania.

Franklin, always proud of his working class roots, became a successful newspaper editor and printer in Philadelphia. He also partnered with William Goddard and Joseph Galloway to publish *The Pennsylvania Chronicle*, a newspaper known for its revolutionary sentiments and criticisms of the British monarchy in the American colonies. He became wealthy publishing *Poor Richard's Almanack* and *The Pennsylvania Gazette*. He played a major role in establishing the University of Pennsylvania and was elected the first president of the American Philosophical Society.

In 1727, Franklin, then 21, created the Junto, a group of like minded aspiring artisans and tradesmen who hoped to improve themselves while they improved their community. The Junto was a discussion group for issues of the day and soon gave rise to many organizations in Philadelphia. Reading was a great pastime of the Junto, but books were rare and expensive. The members created a library, initially assembled from their own books. This was not enough, however, and the search for new books to expand their collection was a source of its main activities from then on.

Franklin then conceived the idea of a subscription library, which would pool the funds of the members to buy books for all to read. This was the birth of the Library Company of Philadelphia: its charter was composed by Franklin in 1731. In 1732, Franklin hired the first American librarian, Louis Timothee, to manage the collection. Originally, the books were kept in the homes of the first librarians, but in 1739 the collection was moved to the second floor of the State House of Pennsylvania, now known as Independence Hall. In 1791, a new building was built specifically for the library, which is now a great scholarly and research library with rare books, pamphlets, and manuscripts, and thousands of graphic items of historical memorabilia.

In 1728, Franklin set up a printing house with Hugh Meredith and the following year became the publisher of a newspaper called *The Pennsylvania Gazette*. The *Gazette* gave Franklin a forum for agitation about a variety of local reforms and initiatives through printed essays and observations. Over time, his commentaries and his adroit cultivation of a positive image as an industrious and intellectual young man earned him a great deal of social respect. He habitually signed his letters with the unpretentious *B. Franklin, Printer*.

In 1733, Franklin began to publish the famous *Poor Richard's Almanack* under the pseudonym Richard Saunders. Though it was no secret that Franklin was the author, his Richard Saunders character repeatedly denied it. *"Poor Richard's Proverbs,"* adages from this almanac, such as "A penny saved is twopence dear" (often misquoted as "A penny saved is a penny earned") and "Fish and visitors stink in three days" remain common quotations to this day. Wisdom in folk society meant the ability to provide an apt metaphor for any occasion, and Franklin's readers became well prepared. He sold about 10,000 copies per year, a circulation equivalent to nearly 3 million now.

Benjamin Franklin at midlife.

In 1758, he ceased writing for the *Almanack* and printed *Father Abraham's Sermon*, also known as *The Way to Wealth*. Franklin's autobiography, begun in 1771 but published after his death, has become one of the classics of the genre. Daylight Saving Time (DST) is often attributed to a 1784 satire that Franklin published anonymously, but DST was first proposed by George Vernon Hudson in 1895.

Franklin's inventions also included social innovations, such as **paying it forward**. Franklin's fascination with innovation could be viewed as altruistic, because he wrote that his scientific works were to be used for increasing efficiency and human improvement. One such improvement was his effort to expedite and promote news services through his printing presses.

In 1747, he retired from printing and went into other businesses. He created a partnership with his foreman, David Hall, which provided Franklin with a tidy percentage of the shop's profits for 18 years. This lucrative arrangement provided leisure time for study, and in a few years he made many scientific discoveries that gave him a reputation with educated persons throughout Europe and especially in France.

Franklin published his *Gulf Stream Chart* in 1770 in England, where it was completely ignored. Subsequent versions were printed in France in 1778 and the US in 1786. The original British edition of the chart was so thoroughly ignored that everyone assumed it was lost forever, until Phil Richardson, a Woods Hole Oceanographer and Gulf Stream expert, discovered it in the Bibliothèque Nationale in Paris. This find received front page coverage in the New York Times.

Benamin Franklin's colorful life and legacy of scientific and political achievement have seen him honored on coinage and money; warships; the names of many towns, counties, educational institutions and companies. He is considered to be the father of modern publishing to this day.

Modern Printing - Invented by William Blake in about 1788, aquatint printmaking uses acid-resistant resin to achieve tonal effects. A similar process to etching, but printed as a relief print, it is the "white" background areas which are exposed to the acid, and the areas to print "black" which are covered with ground. Blake's exact technique remains controversial, but he is known to have used the technique to print texts and images together.

Lithography (from the Greek - *graphein*, "to write") is a method for printing using a stone or a metal plate with a completely smooth surface. The process was invented by Alois Senefelder in 1796 as a low cost method of publishing theatrical works, and can be used to print text or artwork onto paper or another suitable material by using an image drawn in wax or other oily substance as the medium to transfer ink to the printed sheet. The flat surface of the plate or stone is slightly roughened, or etched, and divided into regions that accept a film of water and thereby repel the ink, and others that repel water and accept ink because the surface tension is higher on the image area which remains dry.

Most books were printed using offset lithography from then on and the process became the most common form of printing production until the end of the 20th century.

An example of an aquatint. The colors are vibrant and the detail remains precise with every copy.

Other processes of reproduction became popular during the 19th century. Like etching, each was a labor intensive process.

Chromolithography is a method for making multicolor prints. This type of color printing stemmed from the process of lithography. Printers sought to find a way to print on flat surfaces with the use of chemicals instead of relief or intaglio printing. This process became the most successful of several methods of color printing developed by the 19th century.

Although Senefelder recorded plans for chromolithography, printers in other countries, such as France and England, were also trying to find a new way to print in color. Godefroy Engelmann of Mulhouse in France was awarded a patent on chromolithography in July of 1837, but there are disputes over whether the method was already in use before this date. Other methods were developed by printers such as Jacob Christoph Le Blon, George Baxter and Edmund Evans, and mostly relied on using several woodblocks with the colors.

The technique involved the use of multiple lithographic stones, one for each color, and was still extremely expensive when done for the best quality results. Depending on the number of colors present, a chromolithograph could take months to produce. However much cheaper prints could be produced by reducing both the number of colors used and the refinement of the detail in the image. Cheaper images, like advertisements, relied heavily on an initial black print on which the colors were then overprinted.

To make an expensive reproduction print as what was once referred to as a *chromo*, a lithographer, with a finished painting in front of him, gradually created and corrected the many stones using proofs to look as much as possible like the painting in front of him, sometimes using dozens of layers.

Rotary drum printing was invented by Richard March Hoe in 1843, perfected in 1846, and patented in 1847. Today, there are three main types of rotary presses; offset, commonly known as web offset, rotogravure, and flexo (short for flexography). While the three types use cylinders to print, they vary in their method.

Offset lithography uses a chemical process in which an image is chemically applied to a plate, generally through exposure of photosensitive layers on the plate material.

Gravure is a process in which small cells or holes are etched into a copper cylinder which is filled with ink.

Flexography is a relief system in which a raised image is created on a typically polymer based plate.

Development of the *offset press* came in two versions: in 1875 by Robert Barclay of England for printing on tin cans, and in 1903 by Ira Washington Rubel of the United States for printing on paper. The technique called for the inked image to be transferred (or "offset") from a plate to a rubber blanket, then to the printing surface. When used in combination with the lithographic process, which is based on the repulsion of oil and water, the offset technique employed a flat *planographic* image carrier on which the image to be printed received the ink from ink rollers, while the non-printing area attracts a water based film, keeping the non-printing areas clean.

In printing and typography, *hot metal typesetting* refers to 19th-century technologies for typesetting text in letterpress printing. This method injects molten type metal into a mold that has the shape of one or more glyphs. The resulting sorts and slugs are later used to press ink onto paper.

Different approaches to mechanized typesetting were independently developed in the late 19th century. One, known as the *monotype* system, produced texts with the aid of perforated paper ribbons and cast letters. These machines could produce texts also in "large composition" up to 72 point. Other types of typesetting included Linotype, Typograph, and Monoline.

As was discussed before, screen printing was first patented in England by Samuel Simon in 1907. It was originally used as a popular method to print expensive wall paper, printed on linen, silk, and other fine fabrics. Western screen printers developed guilds and social discipines intended to keep their knowledge and techniques secret.

Early in the 1910s, several printers experimenting with photoreactive chemicals, glues and gelatin compounds. Roy Beck, Charles Peter and Edward Owens studied and experimented with emulsions for making stencils. This trio of developers would prove to revolutionize the commercial screen printing industry by introducing these stencils to the industry, though the acceptance of this method would take many years. Commercial screen printing now uses far safer and less toxic emulsions and photosensitive films, though the basic techniques remain the same.

Joseph Ulano founded the industry chemical supplier Ulano and in 1928 created a method of applying a lacquer soluble stencil material to a removable base. This stencil material, called Rubylith, was cut into shapes, the print areas removed and the remaining material adhered to mesh to create a sharp edged screen stencil.

Screen printing was eventually adopted by artists as a medium for duplication well before the 20th century. It remains popular both in fine arts and in commercial printing, where it is commonly used to print images on Posters, T-shirts, hats, CDs, DVDs, ceramics, glass, polyethylene, polypropylene, paper, metals, and wood.

A group of artists who later formed the National Serigraphic Society coined the word *serigraphy* in the 1930s to differentiate the artistic application of screen printing from the industrial use of the process. *Serigraphy* is a combination word from the Latin word *Seri* (silk) and the Greek word *graphein* (to write or draw).

Following this development came a series of patent disputes and proprietary innovations from companies devoted entirely to the printing process which I will discuss briefly here because they do not figure prominently in the history of book printing apart from their contribution to the modern forms of digital printing we see today: dye-sublimation (1957) and phototypesetting (1960s); the development of the dot matrix printer in 1964; laser printing (1969); thermal printing (1972); inkjet printing (1976); stereolithography (1986); and the digital press in 1993.

With the advent of the digital press, and photoimaging processes made more convenient with the progress of computer processing, the ease of self publishing improved. Publishing houses devoted to making the printing of books a complete system soon took prominence, until we now have a whole series of such houses coming into direct competition with the "traditional" publishing houses, which still rely on the more dated methods of printing and distribution. The result has been an explosion of literature and texts from anyone with a story to tell or a question to explore and share with others.

This brings me back to the premise of this book. I have explained how the process of printing began in order to acquaint you with the advantages you have now.

In the 21st century you are not limited to the traditional way of producing books. You can write a book and bring it to the reader in a tangible or digital form yourself. As methods of storage and distribution of books become even more convenient to the author, there is the potential for an explosion of knowledge and thought, story ideas and dissemination of facts as well as beliefs. The traditional publishing houses are no longer the sole gatekeepers of the common meme.

These publishing methods also carry a certain amount of risk. With the digital age there is less permanence. There is no guarantee that a book will be readable when it is stored on a disc, or a flash drive, or a desktop computer, or even a cell phone or ereader. One has to use electricity to drive these devices, so it is imperative that we find ways to keep the energy we need available. That is why many self-publishing authors value the relative permanence of a physical book. But we can effectively preserve books for posterity without sacrificing trees by making them printable on demand instead of storing them in vast warehouses or keeping large inventories in our garages.

As you read this book I will introduce you to the concepts I learned on my own from experimentation and research. Take them as my way of *paying it forward*, and use them as you will.

YOUR PROJECT

First of all you have to have written a story. If you do not have one ready to print none of the rest of this book will be of particular use to you. It is not enough to simply write something down on paper or type it into your laptop. In order to publish a book you have to have a manuscript to work with. There are several rules that all authors need to obey in order to publish and market a successful book. If you have not done all these things, your book will not be saleable in the public marketplace or even presentable to a professional agent or publisher should you choose that route.

What kind of book can you write? If you have the desire to write but no ideas, I suggest you sit down somewhere and think about it. The quest for knowledge and entertainment is the force behind every book, no matter what it may be about. Let me give you a list of the kinds of books you may want to write:

Fiction: fantasy, science fiction, romance, historical fiction, alternative history, military or war stories, horror, speculative fiction, children's books, fairy tales, biblical or christian fiction, paranormal romance, mysteries, poetry.

Nonfiction: history, cookbooks, philosopy, religion, politics, guidebooks, infoproducts, textbooks, reference books, art books, photobooks, science, sociology, psychology, essays, memoirs, biography, or autobiography.

Some authors like myself can blur the demarkation lines and blend some or all aspects of each into the narrative. When I write a fictional story, I like to do a little research about some feature of the background for the characters, and then discuss it in a few brief paragraphs to enrich the setting based on actual history. When I write nonfiction, I can and do speculate about the subject as "wishful" thinking.

But with nonfiction there are several things which will make it a good book: facts, theories with factual arguments to support them, experiments and their results, statistics, and events which actually happened. There is little room for rumor or fallacy in a nonfiction book.

So You've Got A Story To Tell - What I am about to tell you may seem like old stuff but it is important at this stage. How you write the story is just as important as what the story is about. As a writer, you are an entertainer just as if you were standing on a stage and performing in a play, only your stage is an open book and your props are your writing style and consistency of narrative.

You need to look outside of yourself and your immediate environment in order to attract the attention of the reading public. What are you trying to say with your writing? Do you have a poetic slant, or are you more nuts and bolts in your approach? What is the thrust or aim of your writing; fiction or nonfiction? Is your book about a specific subject, or the compilation of emotional writing or exerpts from your personal journal?

Your work is not only the expression of your soul, it is a mark of your professionalim, so you have to pay close attention to every part of the publishing process, including the preparation and presentation of your manuscript.

Presenting science or factual history *without* doing the proper research is a no-no. A thorough understanding of the subject matter is necessary to create a credible article or plot. Fiction must obey the same rules as science does; that is, the reality of fiction is that the facts are as they are. The challenge is in bending the facts to include the possibility or probability that something can occur without violating, for example, the laws of physics. Your history must be based on something which did or might occur. What you do with the event is limited to what you write which is not part of the event itself. You cannot inject characters into history without making them part of it.

I am reminded of the rule for a Renaissance Faire. If you wear a costume of the period, you cannot wear a wristwatch and have it be visible to others, otherwise you would ruin the effect of "living history". That is an unwritten but time honored rule. Look up the word *anachronism.*

But if you write something like *A Connecticut Yankee in King Arthur's Court* (Mark Twain), you can inject a modern character into the context of medieval legend. The relevent characters continue to behave as they did during that time, and since Arthur was himself a "fictional" historical character (the jury is still out about him) there is no violation of history's rules and you can be just as creative as you want to be.

However, if you employ *text messaging* code or other "shortcuts" to craft your story it will not matter how great it is; it may not pass an editor, and it may never sell as a serious book. The vast majority of readers today, having sat through a standard English class, will find it both jarring and amateurish.

If you employ *slang* or colloquial speech to describe your characters or as part of the narrative, a similar response may occur. If you intend to portray a deliberate style like that in the manner of authors like Anthony Burgess or James Joyce, kudos to you; but be aware that if you couch *all* the books you write in a similar style your lack of literacy will prevent you from being taken seriously as an author. You must employ commonly accepted language with your intended readers when writing your narrative.

Very important components to writing a book: spelling, grammar, syntax, punctuation, voice, and flow.

Phrasing is important, and if you employ the wrong syntax the meaning of a word or phrase can be lost. Often all it takes is a comma put in the wrong place. Inflection and use of terminology are important elements along with the *voice* of the narration. When I speak of voice, I am not only referring to the style of a character's speech but the narrative style of the whole book.

For example, if you are writing a novel of a time in history it is important to couch the dialogue (and sometimes the narrative) in the language of the period. In the 21st century it is now acceptable to adopt what is called the *quasihistoric* voice, which is a modernized version of archaic dialogue without the biblical *thees* and *thous*. I used this model in my pirate/vampire book *A Pirate's Daughter*. The dialogue is colored by the language, grammar and syntax of the period, but not the heavily inflected style of the English language in use at that time. Also, common slang of the time was used sparingly as there was no time to explain to the reader what the words mean. The reader may be able to catch their meaning within context, but too much use of such terms could cause confusion and a loss of interest.

This also speaks to the *flow* of the narrative; that is, the way the words string together into a cohesive whole, with both a rhythm and cadence which call attention to the story's impact. You need to keep the reader interested in the story from beginning to end, so too many details may spoil the soup. If you fall in love with a particular detail when writing use editing to tailor it, or cut it out altogether, especially if it is not critically important to the flow of the plot. This is also true for nonfiction articles and books about a single subject.

And do not forget to make sure your facts are right. Nonfiction carries a different set of rules, and your work will be read by others who may have the expertise you do not. They will be highly critical of your work if you cannot justify your theories with facts to support them.

Here I must talk about a concept which may seem new but which has recently been given a new glossary term. It is called *platform*, or the backstory. When you begin to write a series of books of a particular kind, you must include elements of your platform in them. I use this to keep lines of common elements or the theme of a series. It is a mythology of the story line, which is often explained in each book in various ways. It keeps each book in sync with every other book and guides the reader toward the basic origins of the series without actually going into too much detail in each. A platform can also keep the reader interested in the whole series, so that as one book is read, the reader will be tempted to read the next.

A *series* is not necessary to unify a group of books. Lately, I have found series to be distracting and sometimes a detriment. Even if one book precedes another, around a specific group of characters or backstory, one needs not gather them into a series. That creates a burden on the reader to purchase all the books, and sometimes that is a deal killer. The choice is up to you.

Be sure to read other people's books to get a sense of the style and language they used. Take note of phrasing or poetic prose which will help you to craft emotion in a scene, or listen carefully to the style and pacing of a scene in a movie. Sometimes great lines or quotations can give flavor to your story when used judiciously in the right context. You are not an author until you learn to write to engage the reader's interest and entertainment, so it is vitally important that you read other writers' works. Besides, you never know what you might learn, not to mention the ideas their stories may evoke for future writing.

Remember that dialogue alone without any cogent description of the environment or world the characters live in will leave people thinking your style shallow and expressionless. People need a background to relate to, so describe it in as much detail as you can where it is appropriate. Do not expect them to read your mind.

It is not enough to have written a book without learning the rules other authors use. But do not start out by trying to break them. They are there for a reason.

Edit, Edit, Edit. Lather, rinse, repeat - The flow of ideas may have been relatively easy to put down or very hard, but the most important process for creating a good book is to edit the manuscript. I do not care if you think it's good enough as it is. If you are proud of your idea, your story, or the quality of your writing, it is not finished yet until you go over the whole thing and weed out the mistakes. If you are smart, and I think you are, you will be editing your book every time you finish a chapter or section. Begin at the beginning, or at whichever paragraph you thought was giving you the most trouble.

The most important books you will need to edit your book are:

A dictionary. It does not matter whose; *Merriam Webster, Oxford American, Webster Abridged*. A misspelled word can stand out like a red flag in a cornfield. Even the most seasoned writer has flubbed from time to time. Learn what a word means before you use it, otherwise your reader will not understand what you mean in its use. If you find a single word which conveys your meaning more simply than two, do not be afraid to use it.

A thesaurus. Useful for finding different words from the usual way to say something. Antonyms and synonyms are creative and can also convey a better meaning for a concept than the root word. Adjectives are valuable as descriptive enrichment. You can use the classical *Roget Thesaurus* or the *Webster Thesaurus* for this. I happen to own an *Oxford American Dictionary and Thesaurus*, two books in one.

Three other books which are important for editing are:

The Elements of Style by William Strunk Jr. and E.B. White;

The Elements of Grammar by Margaret Shertzer; and

The Elements of Editing : A Modern Guide for Editors and Journalists by Arthur Plotnik.

If you cannot afford to hire an outside editor to look over your manuscript, they are the best tools you can have to fix any problems your story may have. These books are available in any bookstore. The last book is especially useful in guiding the writer to craft a better book by pointing out the pitfalls most authors are likely to face when reviewed by a professional editor.

Note: if you have *spell checker* embedded in your word processing software (any brand), do not rely too heavily on that function alone. There are many words in the English language which are not contained in the spell checker's dictionary. It will also offer you word substitutions out of context and even replace them automatically, so it is less than useless in any case. Only by learning words and what they mean can help your spelling and enrich your vocabulary. Do not ignore this part of the process. It is vitally important for you to have a clear grasp of spelling, grammar and syntax, and the use of words in context, in order to craft a better story.

Edit for style. Here is one aspect of editing that you need to pay particular attention to. Aside from the rules for writing which I discussed above, you must read your manuscript from beginning to end at least once to determine if the flow reflects your style. This also speaks to *voice.* If you were hasty in writing various sections of the plot and forgot which voice or tense you were using, this is where you can regain it and even the flow. Remember that a consistent flow of narrative is necessary to keep the reader centered in the plot, and switchbacks of style or lack of *continuity* can be jarring. Continuity makes for an interesting and impactful story.

Edit the final product. Once you have caught all the mistakes you think you had made, read it over once again. I have read and edited my stories as many as 15 times before I am satisfied that it is good enough to publish. And in some cases I may decide later that the finished work could stand some trimming or expansion. You are writing both for your reader and for yourself, so do not be afraid to change things if you think they are not good enough. Perfection is a worthy goal, but do not drive yourself crazy with this. Nothing is etched in stone.

You can also ask one of your teachers or a college professor to read the manuscript over for you. There is nothing wrong with getting as much feedback as you can before you can declare your work finished.

There is also no harm in seeking criticism as long as you are prepared to receive it. Criticism helps you to see the things you missed because you are editing inside your own head. What you may think is a brilliant idea may turn out to be a real clunker because your ego did not take your audience, *the reader*, into account.

But beware of criticism which comes from people who *a*) have not actually read the whole story; or *b*) criticize for the sake of criticism alone. Constructive criticism can be very helpful, but criticism which demeans the author or his work for its own sake is not. There are those who enjoy tearing down other people's work just to read their own words. They are called "trolls". Blow them off.

Do not allow others' opinions to sway your decisions too much, or you will lose control of your work altogether. A famous celebrity once said, "*I do not know what defines success, but I know if I try to please everybody I will fail.*" Concentrate on pleasing yourself, and success will follow.

Another approach to editing is to walk away and do something else for a while, then come back and read it fresh. You would be surprised how much better your work will be once you do that. I often read my manuscripts over after having allowed some time to pass. I have occasionally thrown out a whole chapter because I liked it so much while I was writing it. But does the chapter help or detract from the flow of the narrative? A story should proceed in as straight a line as possible. Anything which does not advance the story should be kept out. Copy the extraneous prose out to another file for use later in another book. If you change your mind and want to put it back, it will still be there.

This habit was suggested by one of the most prolific and famous science fiction authors I have known, Harlan Ellison. After reading from his short story *Shatterday* at a science fiction convention, he talked about the way he wrote fragments down on index cards or notebooks and saved absolutely everything for use later. You will not lose any of the great stuff you have written if you adopt the same basic routine and rigorous attention to detail. You can edit out whatever you write secure in the knowledge that all of it will be put to use somewhere else;

if not in the present book, possibly the next. These days, it is as simple as typing the notes into a word editor like Notepad or WordPad and saving it in your digital files.

Above all, do not second guess yourself into writer's block because you're too worried something will not fit. Write in as natural a flow as you are used to. The rest can be worried about later.

Polish your manuscript. If you think you were finished with editing by now, you are not. Once all the dings and gaffs have been edited out and your story has been shaped into a thing of beauty, the polish is the best way to put your best foot forward as an author. The polishing wax is a critical eye, and the polishing cloth is a ruthless wit and a narrow focus. The polish trims off all the unnecessary parts, helps you to see your weakest points, and makes the story end with a satisfying bang. The best way to know when the polish is complete is when you can read your own story from beginning to end and ask yourself, "who wrote this? It's great!"

No book is complete without a great title. After all, you are trying to attract as many readers as you can, so a title is one of the most important parts of the book. If you can sum up the content in a single sentence or phrase, what would it be? A title can convey what a book is about without another word said, and must grab a reader's attention long enough to make him or her pick the book up and look at it. In the case of online sales, the popularity or ranking of a book is dependent solely on the number of copies sold, but do not pay too much attention to that. Your book will sell itself when enough people buy it and share its existence to others, so choose your title carefully with that in mind.

There are occasions when a title might not work with the story. You can change the title whenever you wish.

A note about the duplication of titles. Like ideas, titles are not copyrightable. If you came up with a great title for your story, and you happen to come across the same title by a different author, it is alright to use it anyway. In fact, I have written books which had the same titles as other authors' because that title describes the story best for me. By the same token, there have been other authors who used the same titles as me. If your gut tells you that you cannot find a better title, use it anyway. The plot and the book's cover will erase any confusion between one book and another.

Presenting Your Manuscript To a Publisher

In the 21st century, nothing appears more difficult than getting an agent to represent you to a "traditional" publisher. And there are many agents who say that they are starting to reject submissions of manuscripts due to the vagaries of the current publishing environment, including the uncertainty that a given publisher will still be there the next day. Yet it is possible to get representation if you happen to write nonfiction or fiction books on popular topics.

The main difficulty is in presenting fiction of certain particular types. Children's fiction remains the hot commodity, while science fiction and fantasy, while popular, are slowly losing to the pile of other kinds of fiction like romance and erotica. This even in the face of such films as *Avatar*, which is about as SF/fantasy as you can get.

As I discussed before, the importance of creating a great story is paramount. If you really love the topic you are writing about, you can still get a good agent with the first few sentences of the story.

If you have even more courage you could approach the publisher directly, as long as you are prepared to read through the legal contract and accept the myriad requirements of the publisher. Some features of the contract may be negotiable, others are not. A few publishers will not even look at your book unless you are willing to accept their contract as is. If that is the case, then you had better be prepared to give up a great deal of your creative control to get the book published and into the marketplace.

There have been isolated instances of authors self-publishing and then allowing a major publisher to issue a reprint. I say isolated because most of the time the publisher will not make the offer unless the book is of literary worth; that is, enough copies have been sold (usually hundreds of thousands to the low millions) to satisfy the publisher's perception that its investment in publication will reap some profit. So do not look forward to that as an expected goal or you will drive yourself crazy.

Once you have secured a good agent or found a publisher, however, you need to pay attention to some basic rules of the road.

Fact: In general, when you submit a manuscript to a publisher it is put into a form which the publisher usually employs to create the book. The publisher wants the manuscript in a form which enables the editor to pick and poke at with his blue pencil. The format can affect the number of pages which are published, while the content remains static or is turned back for further editing. The formats used vary from publisher to publisher and from country to country. You have no control over this aspect. The publisher will use precedence to craft the overall look and feel of the book, and will decide all aspects of its production, most of the time without your approval.

Fact: You also have no control over the cover design, and any traditional publisher which accepts your work has its own staff of artists to create the cover. Aesthetics and artistic style, or your ideas about a cover design, do not come into the picture. On rare occasions a publisher will accept your artwork when it directly relates to the content of a story (like a children's book), but this depends on the individual publisher and its rules of submission. There are no set specifications you can follow in this instance.

Remember that an editor's decisions are *subjective*. The facts do not enter into the process. An editor or reader is human, too, and may accept or reject a story based on the mood he/she is in that day.

The traditional format for a manuscript submitted to a traditional publisher comes in three parts, which I will review here:

The query letter - no manuscript can be presented to the publisher without it. It tells the publisher who you are, what your goal is or why you wrote the book, the title and what the book is about, the number of words and the genre you see it placed in. If the book is part of a series, you can include the titles of the other or following books and a *brief* discussion of the history or inspiration for it.

The standard query letter comprises one page and one page *ONLY*. Publishers do not have the time to read your life history. If it goes longer than that, they may not read it at all and reject your work or set it aside. Once that happens, you can be assured that your labor of love will be buried under new material coming in or forgotten altogether. A few may take the time to send you a nice polite but perfunctory rejection letter.

The synopsis - one to three pages which give a description of the flow of the story, who the main characters are, and a *brief* overview of each chapter. This gives the publisher a basic guide to the important plot segments and shows that it has a beginning, a middle, and an end. Some publishers will accept only one page, so a paragraph or three describing the story and the type of plot – adventure, tragedy, victory, space opera or so on, may be sufficient.

Make your first paragraph the most important by telling the basic story. The rest is really more of a summary of the plot. And be careful writing this document. You will have to edit it just as heavily as your manuscript, because it will show your writing skill as a thumbnail for the whole picture. If you cannot engage the publisher's interest with this, then you have more work to do.

The manuscript or sample chapters - the maximum amount of material to submit is usually *one to three* chapters or the entire manuscript, depending on the submission requirements of the publisher. *Do not send a CD or a whole manuscript by email unless they ask for it*. Generally, most publishers have not caught up with the internet so any attempt to circumvent their procedures for the interest of saving time will not advance your situation any better than by following the rules. If you try to do that and they prefer a mailed box of paper, they will not respond to further contact from you.

A manuscript submitted to a publisher also has a specific format. The title page usually contains the title, your author byline, the number of words and your contact information. The standard type font they like is 12 point Times Roman. This makes for a labor-intensive printing job once your manuscript is finished and ready to present. A medium sized book can take a ream of paper or more to print off, and the cost of shipping should be seen as a capital investment. Do not try to save paper by printing double sided. Use only one side of a sheet. The publisher also needs to know your real name in order to pay you. At no time will they reveal your real name to the public unless you allow it or use your real name as your pen name.

The manuscript page: here is where your manuscript, edited and polished for style, occupies the page: double spaced with 1 inch margins all around and a ragged right margin. Some publishers may ask for justified margins and single spaces between sentences. Be sure to look at their submission requirements *before* you proceed. If you are still not sure, ask.

I know, this can be a pain but if you want to get noticed *you have to follow their rules*. Once you do that, your manuscript will be handed to a reader to examine and recommend it to the managing editor for publication.

Expect to spend a good deal of time waiting for a response. A major publisher receives *thousands* of manuscripts every day, and there is only a small staff to go through the *slush pile* at each. Some authors have waited for up to a year only to receive a polite rejection letter in return. Even if you are lucky enough to secure an agent, the wait can be frustrating. An agent only speeds up the reading period somewhat but the result may still be the same.

But do not be discouraged by this. It is only another roadblock in your fight to be recognized as an author. Keep trying.

Preparing To Publish On Your Own

The same is not true about publishing houses that enable you to self-publish. Each of the online self-help publishers has its own set of trim and format sizes, kinds of paper it uses, and fonts (typefaces) it will accept. Some will accept a raw document file and image file to convert into hard copy files in the form of PDFs (Portable Document Files), which they present to their affiliate printers. They are also quite flexible and will accept your own artwork or give you a selection of generic cover designs to use. Others will *only* accept a PDF, not a document file or image file.

But before you can submit your manuscript for publishing through any one of them, you need to put it into a standard format both on the inside and on the outside. Presuming that you have written your manuscript using a software package like *Word* or *Wordperfect*, you already have the raw file ready to format. But you are not finished with it yet.

The Interior

If your manuscript is still set with a ragged right margin and double spaced, you have to justify your margins and create a document which is single spaced. In *Word*, you do this through the *"Page Setup"* feature and the *"Format"* feature. In applications later than 2003 it is almost automatic but you will have to override some of the autoformat rules which demand you follow the manuscript style by using the Word toolbar. Typefaces will come later.

Set your margins to a standard width, usually .4 or .5 inch all around, and you will have to set your gutter space to a minimum of .5 inch. Most printing services prefer .5 inch. Do not let the gutter space fool you. The text inside the *textblock* will adjust slightly toward the outer edge of the paper depending on the size of the gutter. I find that margins of .3 inch and a gutter size of no less than .5 inch are satisfactory. More space than that (what I call "negative space") will increase the number of pages in the document file and leave less room for the text. Some printers will allow you to set the outside margin at .3 instead of .5 inch. Others prefer a greater margin width and so on, depending on the printing size of your book. Remember that the number of pages in your interior file must be evenly divisible by 2. If you end on an odd page, you must add a blank page to make up the difference.

Set the printing orientation to "*mirror margins*" and the gutter orientation to "*left*". You must select "*whole document*" to make the file uniform in size, margin depth and orientation.

You will need these pages added to finish the product: the *Title* page and the *Copyright* page. Each of these should always be the 1st and 2nd pages anyone sees. The standard used to include an inside flyleaf or blank page before the title page, but the difference can mean an increase in the corresponding number of pages for the whole book, and most modern printing machines do not recognize that blank page.

If you find that you must add a blank page, you can set one the end of the textblock. This means the *total* number of pages in the book's interior is the total for your metadata information. Note that the *total* number of pages in the document file is what is counted, not the number of pages with page numbers. This includes the blank pages. This is why you must pay attention to your page spacing and your margins.

The title page. Look at the title page at the beginning of this book. The subtitle refers to whatever series the book is in or an extended portion of the title beyond what is listed on a product page. The imprint is the logo or type you put in to identify yourself by your printing house or by your own publishing company. In my case I chose to use my trademark brand and site URL in lieu of my office location on the title page, along with the city where my office is located on the inside copyright page. Look at any book in your library to see how they are used.

The copyright page. Printed on the back of the title page (standard). There are no page numbers or headers to include here either. You do not start adding page numbers until you get to your *Foreword* or *Introduction*. Or, if the foreword is only a paragraph or less than a page you can leave the page numbers off and include them in the main section. For example, if you look at the Introduction in this book you see that the page numbers are Roman numerals. I use them to distinguish between the introduction and the actual beginning of the book. Standard publishers add dedications or memorials on the next page with a blank page added afterward. If there is enough room on your *Introduction* page I would advise adding them there to save paper. Generally, it is up to you to add one or not.

The Table of Contents is optional and also has no page number. For a sample, look at the Table of Contents on the 3rd page of this book. A table of contents is necessary in your nonfiction book as an overview of the chapters or sections contained in it, but is not a requirement in a fiction book. A table of contents may be required when you set up an ebook, but that will be discussed later.

The *textblock.* The actual interior text of your book. It can be divided into sections or occupy a single section, but it must take a uniform appearance throughout the book. You achieve this by presenting it in a standard font and your headlines in another font.

You can format the *vertical alignment* of the text in the alotted space to *"center"*, but that may change the placement of pictures imported to the document file. Pictures which were set in the center but whose border touches the bottom margin may get kicked onto the next page with a huge space in between, so it is best to leave the vertical alignment in that case at *"top"*. For plain text, *"center"* is best except in the case of the last page, where you might have to set it at *"top"* for that page only.

If you are not sure about this, there is a help module set at the end of the main menu in your word processing software which will enable you to see what a page looks like as you set each parameter. In versions of Word after 2007, you may have to save your interior as a lower version of Word in order to render the file compatible. I have Word 2018 but I have the option to create a file designated format 97-2003, which is a pain but will pass through most older publishers' software easily.

Once you have set your parameters for the document, you must then save it as a .doc or .docx which is compliant with the publishing requirements before going on to the next step.

However, since one must now render the file as a PDF for submission to my printer, ensuring compatibility is no longer necessary.

Setting the *header and footer* (usually the title and page numbers) depends on the number of sections in your file and how you want to divide it. Again the help module will give tips on how to do this. I have to warn you that this is the hardest part of finishing the file to prepare it for printing, so do not be surprised if you experience some difficulties. Headers and footers are a special case which I will discuss only briefly here.

The minimum space between a header or footer and the edge of a page is .3 inch and the header and footer rest *inside* the textblock. This is standard. I have used .5 inch on occasion, but that will only reduce the amount of space available on the page for the main body text. It is recommended that the header be set in a smaller type size than the text.

In some older printed books the header was much bigger than the rest of the text, but not aesthetically pleasing to the eye and raised the cost to print. Remember that you must minimize the reader's distraction from the story or article as much as possible, and maximize the space availabe for the textblock. This will save you money in the long run.

You set the header and footer to each section of your document file according to your *Page Setup* or *Layout* feature, and you must be careful to set your page and section parameters accordingly. Everything relates to everything else. The distance of a single linespace can kick the whole section into the next one and you will have to start over again.

The *page number* feature is a little tricky in some versions of Word. It allows you to set the page number independently of the *header and footer* feature, and also to add it and format it in the feature. Be careful that if you use sections to separate your text from your title and copyright pages that you *turn off* the *"same as previous"* first on your header and footer setting where necessary, or the header from the previous section will cover the new section. Remember that the reverse or even page is the mirror image of the odd or front page. You will have to set the odd pages and even pages separately where necessary.

Here I must talk about *economy of space.* As the price of printing goes up due to market and paper supply issues, the greatest amount of information must be able to fit the smallest space to reduce your overall number of pages. This means that your choice of type face, font, size and spacing must be used judiciously along with the choice of book size. Each self-help publishing service offers a variety of what are called *trim* sizes and printing preferences. They also offer a selection of paper colors and weights.

One of the reasons that I use the 6" x 9" *trade paperback* trim size is that I can put a longer book into fewer pages. The price to print goes down proportionally compared to the number of pages used. As the *unit* cost (usually a minimum amount set by the printer) goes down, the *total* cost of printing goes down, and you can set your *list* price (retail price) lower based on the amount of money you want to make from the sale of the book. More about this in the ***How To Price and Sell Your Book*** section.

Spacing is also important. If your book includes sections within sections or chapters, you can reduce the number of pages in the file by resizing the skip lines to 8 points each. This can save you as much as a page or two of textblock throughout the entire document. Another way to save paper is to begin a new chapter two or three line spaces down instead of on the next available page. This way you can shave another ten pages off easily.

The choice of ***type face*** or ***font*** is also up to you. You can use a font to generate interest in your story, or to set the mood for the reader. There are two kinds of font: serif (letters with "tails" on them) and sans-serif (letters without tails). The letters are presented in *points per inch.* The smallest available is 8 points, while the largest is 120 points. You can manually force point sizes smaller or larger than these, but this is not recommended. You can also fix the size of the type in pixels instead of points when working with the cover design.

The standard font used in a block of text is *Times New Roman*, but that is a heavy serif type that is hard to read at lower sizes. If you are interested in learning more about alphabet fonts and their design, I recommend you get a book about typefaces or experiment with the typefaces available through your image or word processing software. There are usable fonts available online if you type in the word "fonts" in your web browser. Some are subject to copyright but most are copyright free. You download them and then install them into your standard "fonts" file, which is contained on your C:// drive.

Printer settings may require that headlines or decorative type be *embedded* in your document file, or created as separate image files and then inserted into the file as part of the text. Because your self-help publisher's printers may not support the particular font you want to use, you must choose what you think conforms to their list or their processing software may read it as another font in its own database and replace it automatically.

In *Word*, you can set the document to embed the fonts by looking for it in the *Tools* format feature, go to the advanced preference section *Options*, go to the *Save* tab and check the *Embed True Type fonts* box. Depending on which version of software you use, there is also a help guide. Use it instead of guessing. It is up to you to contact your printing service and get this information for your software before you start because it will prevent a lot of headaches and confusion later on.

Even then, there are no guarantees this will generate an interior the publisher can print. You have no idea how many people I have seen complain in forums that they cannot get this or that thing to happen, when all they had to do was look for the instruction manual and follow it.

Another option is to create images of titles or section titles and insert them into the file at the place you have marked for them. In all cases, be sure that the print resolution for each image is at least 300 dpi. Some printer will accept JPGs, others will demand you use TIFs, PNGs or even Bitmaps. Be sure to check with your service first.

Inserting photos and/or illustrations: Depending on the size of the source file, it may be possible to insert a picture at its original size, but doing so only increases the **total size** of the whole file. If you are going to upload the file to an online printer the size of the pictures will slow the time to upload considerably. Most online publishers will not allow uploads of files bigger than 200MB, so if your document is needlessly large it may not upload at all.

To save space, set the width of the largest pictures to .9 of the width of the textblock so that they will fit exactly within the margins, or make them slightly smaller and center them on the document. You will need picture manipulation software to modify or reduce it.

I recommend *Adobe Photoshop* for this, though if you have a *Thumbs+* or *Paint Shop* program you can also use it to resize the picture. *Adobe Photoshop CC* is the version I use now, and it can do everything; though it can get a little pricey at first. It functions in the cloud, so you can download and install it without backup discs. Updates are sent periodically, so if you have any problems, updates will repair the program. Any good software from your computer dealer will suffice, but most will recommend Adobe. The latest version can also process CMYK files, which is now the standard for color printing. Other solutions for Apple products will have similar settings.

In **Word**, which is my document processor, you can insert images and can click on the inserted image to adjust the size, brightness, contrast, and change it from color to grayscale with *Picture Format* or *Resize*. You can even give it a border and place it in a table, insert tables of pictures and text together, and other layout features. This saves time, and you do not have to bother with switching back and forth between your image processor and the document processor.

However, you should have processed your image files to the requisite size and format first before inserting them into your document file. **The required printer resolution for a picture is 300 dpi or more for printed books.** A subsitute can be a TIF or PNG file which is an uncompressed image format, and saved without a color index (ICC) code.

You can also multitask by running both programs at once, and then you will have the full capability of a document engine at all times. But be careful with this: if you resize an image smaller in Word it will take the resolution down below 300dpi. You are better off resizing the image in your imaging software and reinsert it where you want it to go. Pay attention to the number of dots per inch (printer resolution), and the width and height in pixels (screen resolution). One is not the same as the other.

In the case of *ebooks* you can get away with 150 dpi by increasing the contrast a notch or two. As long as you set the width of a picture in inches to slightly less than the width of the textblock, it will fit whether it is set to 72 dpi or 600 dpi. The ratio of pixels to inches will be retained.

If you have an illustration or photo which is half the size of the textblock on a given page, you can create a table where text can flow past it, saving another 1/3 of a page. The use of tables is especially important where you want to have a paragraph or caption text set next to your image, or a series of images lined up together in an orderly fashion. However, your printer/publisher may demand that you use inline insertions instead.

Just remember this: ***never resize a small picture to a larger size*** *in a Word document*. Depending on its original size, enlarging may result in loss of data, pixilation, and blurriness. Some image formats do not resize well like *jpg, png*, and *bmp*. A *Tiff* or TIF (tagged image file) can be resized in most image software programs to a certain extent, but if it is converted from a smaller *jpeg* or *bmp* file the same result will occur. It is always best to start with a picture with large dimensions at a high printer resolution, then reduce it as needed in other software before insertion. *.bmp* is large, primitive and totally uncompressed. The size of a bitmap file can boost the overall size of an interior file hundreds of times, so I have found it adequate to use a PNG or TIF.

Another rule of thumb is: never use a TIF file when a JPG will do. Jpeg image files are compressed, so there is some loss of resolution data if you use them in place of truer sized files, but they are preferred by some publishers. If they ask for JPGs, use them. If they ask for TIF files, use them. Do not fudge the details. You should consult the FAQ of your own publishing service to make the image compatible with their requirements.

In certain instances the images produced have proven better than the originals; but your software may not be as flexible as mine. Be sure to test the software before you proceed, as I cannot guarantee your results will be the same. I have experimented extensively to get the best results. Be sure that you do the same so that you are familiar with the advanced features as well as the limitations of the software you are working with.

In all cases you must follow these basic rules in order to make your book ready for publication and to avoid headaches later on. If you are preparing the book for distribution, the distribution monitor will look it over to see if the basic standards have been met. *They will kick it back to you to make these corrections if you do not.* You must *never* assume that they will let these irregularities slide by.

I know of other authors who uploaded a file to the printer engine and did not look the source file over for gaffs, nor did they look at the PDF (final form) to catch mistakes before they approved the book. This caused them to spend time correcting the mistakes, then having to purchase another proof copy. Revisions are also both unnecessary and expensive, so to avoid them double check your final product before you approve it.

In summary, these are considered standard for printing the file you are going to submit:

1. The number of pages to print must be evenly divided by 2 (standard). If you have a story which fills 75 pages, your file must include a blank page on the back to make up the difference. If your book must be divisible by 4, the printer will insert blank pages. You will still have to pay for the total number of pages to get the book printed.

2. Margins must be **equal** at .3 to .5 inch, **mirror margins** (except in the case of ebooks, where you expect to read them on *Kindle* or other ereading device. More about that later).

3. Text is *justified* (text set flush to both margins) and *single spaced.* Exceptions are acceptable for indented paragraphs and/or special features like pictures, but all must occupy the inside of the text area. Paragraph tabs are set at a minimum of .25 inch. The gutter is set at a *minimum* of **.5 inch** or a maximum of **.9 inch,** *left.*

4. Headers and footers set at a *minimum* of **.3 inch**, type size smaller than text. These are optional. If you want to save more file space or your book is a novel, leave the header out and resize your page numbers to a smaller font.

5. Pictures resized to fit the text area at 90-100%. The best printer resolution to use is a minimum of **300 dots per inch** (dpi). Some publishers may require an even higher printer resolution, and in specific formats like GIF, PNG, or TIF. But unless they specify the format, one can get away with a JPG in most cases.

The Cover

When submitting a book to a self-help publisher, you are free to explore your own options in order to prepare your cover for publication. In general, you want the images you create for the cover to be of the best quality and the finest resolution. The basic design for a good book cover contains a few critical elements which I will discuss here. If you are already skilled at being a cover artist, you should review this part so that you can improve your designs. These are not requirements. They are mere guidelines.

There are three basic parts to a book cover: **the front, the spine,** and the **back.**

A traditional publisher hires an artist to produce a cover which will catch the buyer's eye quickly and create an interest in the book. The type of cover or its design will be determined by what is called the *target market* for the subject of the book, be it fiction or nonfiction. If the book is nonfiction, sometimes all that is needed is the title and author's name on the front, with a smaller image or font which conveys the slant the author is aiming for.

A simple cover can consist solely of the title and author name. This is what I call the fallback style of cover. It is especially useful when you are producing ebooks and want to embed the cover in the reading file.

Depending on what kind of book you are writing, the style of cover is critical. In some cases, a quirky title is not enough to attract interest. You have to point it out in bright colors or with a specialty font or title design.

In all cases, the cover must contain the three basic elements; *the title, the author's name,* and a *subtitle* if necessary. If you are not inclined to bother with all of it, self-publishing services like Lulu or CreateSpace will offer you a basic designer which will help you create a decent cover in a few minutes.

I happen to use Ingram Spark, a subsidiary of Lightning Source which prefers PDF or In Design submissions, but as an artist I don't need this feature.

The placement of these elements is also critical. For examples, study the covers of books in a bookstore, or experiment with doodling.

Your choice of font should be attention grabbing, and the insert relevent to the topic. You may be able to convey the theme of the book with just a few simple elements. In another instance one is able to insert a small photograph, symbol or a design, surrounded by the relevent type.

There are important features to preparing the cover which may be created using a template which is downloaded to you as a PDF or InDesign File, depending on which program you are using. The template will usually be 15″ x 12″, in CMYK or Grayscale and 16 bits/channel. Don't worry about this. You will be inserting your TIF cover files onto this template.

The usual front cover of a paperback book goes to the trim edge of the paper and has a standard *bleed* area of 1/8 inch, or .125 inch, added onto the original size of the cover. So for a 6″ x 9″ trade paperback book the front cover dimensions are 6.127″ x 9.25″, with the design couched against the left edge of the area. This leaves 1/8 inch to trim off. To be safe I would figure for an extra 1/16 inch of space along the right and left edges of the design so that the ¼ inch margin is preserved. If you do not pay attention to this your title may not print at center, and part of the design may be cut off.

I remember an artist who wanted to design a cover around a book about a massacre in a Colorado high school. She had produced quite a good one, with a few bloodstains and a photograph of the high school against a background filled with words. But the words were grey. They could not possibly compete with the bloodstains for attention. I suggested that she highlight the words in dark red and the most important ones in bold type so that they would stand out. When she did this, her cover had more significance. People wanting to read about the tragedy could see the theme of the book outlined on the cover.

Image copyright 2012

Here, a compelling photograph forms the background for a simple title block. If you prefer you can carry the whole photograph to the top and superimpose the title on it. But remember not to allow too many details to clutter it up. The title and the author's name are the most important elements.

The photo may convey the mood or the subject of the book, but it is decorative more than anything else. Many readers are attracted to good cover design so bear this in mind.

A full treatment with artwork tailored to the actual plot of the book, sometimes related to the main character or theme of the story. This one happens to be one of my own.

The spine is where you put the title, author and publisher name; and the calculator will advise whether you have room to put text on it. Again, there is a margin for space of 1/16 inch on the left and right edges where the printer expects the type will not go. As with a typical text page the top and bottom margins should be 1/4 to 3/8 inch. For a spine width of 1/2 inch or less, it is recommended that you omit the text. Do not worry if there is no text on a narrow spine. In all cases, online sellers will display the front cover anyway, so the absence of text on narrow spines is not important.

The spine text is normally oriented so that it can be read sideways from the top down and so that the front cover is turned up. Depending on the width of the spine you can even turn the text so that it displays horizontally.

A sample of spine text:

Your publishing logo or imprint design can be text alone, an imprint logo or a picture. Here, the spine is just wide enough that I can place my imprint logo so it can be read when the book is turned up. If there is room, you can add the ISBN of the book or some other identifying number. In order for your spine to look the way you want it to, you may have to make the entire cover yourself as one piece or create a spine as a separate item to insert into the master template.

The spine width can be determined from the number of pages to be printed. Usually, the number of pages must be evenly divisible by 2. Some publishers will have a spine width calculator you can use, or will give you a template already prepared to use based on the number of pages in your book's interior. But here is a handy tip. Depending on what kind of paper you are allowed to use, white or cream, there is a way to figure out your spine width.

For white paper, I figure the spine by multiplying the total number of pages in the file by .002252. For cream (crème) paper, I multiply the total number of pages in the file by .0025. The reason for this is that the grade of paper used determines the multiplier. Cream paper is slightly thicker than white, though they are both called 50lb..

If you are being published by a self-help printer like Lulu they may automatically place their logo on your book's spine. You can opt out of that in the preparation phase of the cover creation by unchecking it.

The **back cover** can be completely blank or can contain images and text. The margins are the *mirror image* of the front cover. You can use the back cover to describe what the book is about, whether or not it is part of a series, a small blurb about your publishing company and contact information, as well as the barcode for the ISBN number of the book. Some paperback books display a wrap around design with the title, spine and back elements superimposed.

A barcode *may* be necessary *if* you want to sell the book to bookstores. It is not a *legal* requirement, but some bookstores and major chains will not buy your book for resale without one. If you intend to sell directly through your site or through your publishing service it is not necessary. Some services may supply you with an ISBN so that you will be able to publish the product to their distributors or other affiliates, and they will place the barcode on the cover for you. But be careful with this. Should you want to change publishing services, you will have to republish without their number; so it is safer to buy your own.

Along with your contact information be sure to include the ISBN number on the copyright page. I prefer to group it with the URL of my website on the back cover and with enough room so that my service can insert the barcode.

Notice that the bleed margin and the safety margin are each 1/8 (.125) inch in width just like the front cover. To allow for bleed you will have to resize the design so that the important areas lie inside the safety margin. Any of the colors within should be extended all the way to the edge of the template so there will be no white space left over. This is how you preserve the cleanest edges for trim.

It is important that both the front and back covers be of the same resolution so that the final cover file you generate will be uniform throughout, both in printer resolution and in screen resolution. In all cases, follow the specifications your printing provider gives you, or the cover will not fit the final product. Your printer should also have templates for you to follow so that your cover will fit precisely and look professionlly made. In all cases, figure that the cover design must print at a minimum of 300 dpi or higher. There are no exceptions.

When you produce the cover it must usually be in the form of a *PDF* (Portable Document File) for most publishing services. Some publishers will convert them for free, though you will have to buy a proof copy anyway. There are other publishers that require that you have the cover already converted to their image file specifications, or they will charge extra for the conversion.

Addendum: There are certain standards for publicly allowable content with regard to covers. Overall, the cover must be acceptable to view by all ages of readers. Even if the book is the raunchiest you have ever written, the cover should contain only those elements which make the book buyable, or just the title and author name on the front. If you designed the cover yourself it should contain nothing which can be deemed pornographic or offensive to the general public. When you are dealing with the public *their* sensibilities, not yours, are what you should be paying attention to. When you publish the book the description should also have that information in it, called a disclaimer, on the product page of whatever online seller you choose to sell through.

The fact is that many sites which promote pornography are shut down every day. If you want to avoid this make sure that your book is presentable to the wider audience.

But if you are preparing a wrap around cover for a hardback volume, the dust jacket must be designed as one piece, so the dimensions of your cover design must include the spine and the outside flaps. A dust jacket design includes these flaps so that you can wrap the hard cover book in it to protect the clothbound covers, and so that you can remove it as needed. You can also add biographical information and a photo as well as anecdotal information about the book to them rather than use the back cover. The barcode attached to each book is placed on the back coverpart of the jacket close to the bottom and the inside margin, or sometimes the center or outside margin.

Advanced topic: If you are an accomplished artist as well as a writer you should take note that the use of color in your original piece may not match with the finished product. You may have to convert your image file from one format to another. Many publishing printers still use what is called 4 color separation, especially those who print for the traditional publishers, but they are slowly moving toward digital composition and layout.

In most *Adobe Photoshop* versions after 2009, like *Photoshop Pro* or *CC*, you can convert your color image files from RGB (red-green-blue) to **CMYK** (cyan, magenta, yellow, and black). In other words, you can convert the image from the standard 3-color format to the 4-color printing format. Your home printer uses at least 4 colors of ink to print an image, and some are programmable to print both kinds.

With photoshop processors like *Adobe LE* or *Elements 9*, however, your software may not be able to do this. If you can find an online pamphlet printer who will convert your file to CMYK, I recommend that you use them to prepare your image files properly, or rely on your publishing service to do this for you. *Adobe Photoship CC* can and will convert your image file to CMYK, which is quite a timesaver. However, conversion of the digital file to a PDF may help you skip this process. I use it that way, which is why most if not all of my book covers come out true to color.

Interior art: In all cases, there is a price to be paid for the difference between color and black & white images inserted into a textblock. Color images are more expensive to print and you will be charged extra for the use of the inks when they are printed. Some printers will *only* print black & white interiors *or* color interiors. You cannot mix and match. Also, the finished document file is larger for color interiors and may exceed the 200MB limit for upload. Other printers will allow you to break up the file, which a labor intensive process, so your choice of color vs black & white will determine which way to go.

At a minimum of 300dpi a file appears much larger on your screen than what you see on the printed page. If you are going to publish a book with a lot of images in it, you are better off printing them in *grayscale* or black & white, as I have with this book. If you convert an image to grayscale you are using only 8-16 bits instead of 256K per square inch of space. At certain printing resolutions you might also experience something called a *moire'* pattern for dot screen images, especially if you send in a file with photos that are still formatted in RGB.

Another option is to go ahead and use color images but expand your book into a larger print size to save money on the printing. This will not change the overall size of the document file, but will reduce the number of pages to print.

Still another option is to print both black & white and color images together with the color option, and pay for the whole production as a color project. Keep this in mind if you use halftone images. For example, my book *A BOOK OF FIVE RINGS: A Practical Guide to Strategy by Miyamoto Musashi* is a combination illustrated book containing line drawings, photos and color gallery. The difference in cost came out to be a dollar.

Some self-help publishing services have a strict set of rules about interior images which may disappoint you. Some will *insist* that the optimum size for an image is 300dpi, boosting the overall size of the interior file above what is optimal for uploading. This is why many books which might normally contain lots of illustrations do not.

If you are stuck with this sort of service you may be wise to find another just to print that book, as opposed to wasting time fighting them. Another option is to pay your publisher to print the book in offset format, but that is more expensive than digital printing and requires a minimum print run you may not be able to afford.

There are no such restrictions with **ebooks**. As long as you keep your document file's total size to a maximum of 100MB, you can show color images in your interior file to your heart's content. I had to prepare each one of my books using the rules I outlined in the section above. But more about ebooks later.

The Galley Proof

Once you have set up your document files you now have the ingredients to produce what is called a *galley proof,* or *proof copy.* It is a representative form of what the book is going to look like when it is ready to publish. Some printers will send you a proof as is, while others will insert a blank page on the back of the text file with a barcode to identify it in their system and the word "*Proof*" splashed across it.

Upload your digital files to the printer by means of their portal software, or you can store them on a CD and mail it directly, though that is not always necessary. For Lulu you can upload the files directly to their publishing engine, which is a distiller that converts your raw files into PDFs automatically.

CreateSpace requires PDFs instead of the raw files, but is the cheaper option for getting your book printed without having to give up an arm and a leg in the process. But that is all. Its distribution program is not as sophisticated or professional as that of **Lightning Source**, which is attached directly to Ingram Content Group.

Lighting Source requires that you make the PDFs yourself for upload, and they charge a fee for the setup. However, their attention to detail is what makes them the superior service above all. For a small fee per title, you can be distributed to any bookstore in the world, Amazon, Barnes & Noble, and so on. Occasionally, LSI will promote their service by offering a coupon for the initial setup of a book. Then if you time it right, you can publish a book virtually for free.

In November they offer setups for free as part of NanoWriMo, a period where most authors should be writing and publishing the most heavily before the Christmas gift giving season.

Some publishers limit their book trim sizes deliberately to encourage you to use them exclusively, but they cannot force you to.

Be sure to insert all your information, including your ISBN or catalog number in your copyright page and on the back cover, before submitting the files to be converted into PDFs. You do not have to insert the retail price on the cover, since your book will mostly be sold online and you may want to offer the book at a discounted price. However, some bookstores want a printed price so that they can discount the price to the customer. Your own pocketbook should determine which way to go.

Once that is done the printer will ask you to order a *proof copy*, for which they will charge you the **unit cost** for printing plus shipping and handling. Depending on where you live, they may also charge *use tax*. Since the proof copy is for your use, I recommend you pay the tax, then give them a resale license later to avoid paying it on purchases later on. More about this later.

It is vitally important that you inspect your copy for any gaffs and mistakes which were not detected in the final process. You should have already examined the PDFs before upload, but sometimes printer errors may have resulted, like extra lines or page breaks. First, look over the interior to see if any artifacts like these features appear in the textblock. Even if you edited your text file, the distilling processor may have seen things you did not, and typos appear more easily as a result. If you did not embed your fonts, the proof will show it.

Read the entire text over and compare it with the raw file to make sure that it is exactly the way you laid it out. Make corrections as necessary, then create a new PDF and upload it to revise the book.

Do the same with the cover. This is the time where you get to see the printed result, how it is trimmed and whether things center properly. If the cover does not look exactly like your original file it may have been converted to CMYK in the process (or not), and the color balance may be slightly off. You will have to change the color setting, the balance or the saturation, the brightness and/or contrast to make it more to your liking, then upload it to the distiller or make a new PDF to replace it.

If you have the capacity to print it out, make sure that you do to see how it looks first before you even upload that version. The cover is an important part of your book.

If you are not happy with the results, this is your opportunity to make whatever changes you need to, because once you release it to the booksellers or start selling it yourself your book needs to remain in a final form, especially if you have an ISBN attached to the book. This seals the form of the book as it is until you retire it from sale or revise it. This process can be repeated as many times as required until you are satisfied with the final product.

Note: If you use a service which converts for you, make sure you download the PDFs to keep a copy of both the textblock and the cover for your records. You never know when you might have to move your books from one publisher to another, or if the publisher closes shop or has accidental damages to it. It is also one of the best ways of ensuring your book will be safe.

A word about publishing books in the public domain: if you are considering doing this let me warn you that you are in for a complicated legal entanglement. Not only are they nonsellers, there is already a glut of such books listed on *Google*, *Gutenburg.org*, and other file sharing sites which are in competition with you. The list of authors already pursuing legal action against these sites is enormously long and growing longer every day.

If you have a desire to reprint these books, you must do the proper research and make sure that the books are legal "orphans", or the author has been dead the requisite number of years past the copyright limit (usually 70 years). There may also be estate claims against the legal right to publish, so my advice is: ***don't***. The sake of your continued success as an author or publisher may be at stake.

However, that does not restrict your right to use what has been written already to create an original story or to rewrite the original plot. Just as many filmmakers have a vision to "remake" a given movie or television show, you may find a gem of adaptable material among the tarnished treasures. But your use of this material may not gain you more respect as an original author. If you find that there is a creative justification for this practice, go ahead. Just do not relay too heavily on other people's writing to pad your book, and if you copy too much or too often you could be accused of *plagiarism*. There is creative innovation and there is just plain cheating. Your honesty as a storyteller and a published author are not mutually exclusive.

Publishing Services

I would be remiss if I did not discuss the benefits and drawbacks of using a printing service geared to produce a book. The best of these are in order:

Lightning Source, Inc. (LSI, *www.lightningsource.com*) is a full service publishing service which works with all sorts of publishers and small presses. They are a subsidiary of Ingram Content Group, which distributes most if not all of the books to many bookstores. They will print your books in a variety of formats, but you must provide your own files as finished PDFs. If you do not have an ISBN they will insert a generic barcode for you free of charge to track the book throughout the printing process, but you will not recieve distribution. They offer both digital and offset printing. Offset is printing the old fashioned way of producing a hardback book, so your files will have to be set up for that. They offer a wide range of trim sizes and book sizes, binding styles and special types of books.

They charge a set up fee per title by and prefer credit cards; and also offer a trade credit line for larger print runs. They will accept a cashier's check but that would slow down the process considerably. They also charge for revisions and an annual catalog fee per book, and if you want a proof copy you must pay for it. You must also supply your own ISBNs if you want distribution to the major booksellers. They are willing to work with you if you plan to become a small publisher or have several books to publish.

Recently, LSI has divided itself into two distinct services: one for large and multiple division publishers having 30+ books to publish; and another for small presses as well as individual authors. The latter is called *Ingram Spark*, and has the ability to work the same way as the main branch. But it also publishes ebooks for distribution.

With LSI or Ingram Spark you can have your books set up for sale on Amazon, Barnes & Noble, and many other major booksellers online all over the world in less than a week, as compared to other publishing services. Their customer support is exceptional in that you have a "staff" of representatives to answer your questions every step of the way.

They also give you an operating manual which lists their printing and distribution specifications, access to templates to complete your project, and other guides. These guides and templates are accessible online. They are truly the publisher's publisher and are more professional than many others. However, they do not accept PayPal, so if you do not want to use your credit card you are basically out of luck. For more information, visit their website.

CreateSpace was an Amazon owned company but has been absorbed into their Kindle Direct Publishing (KDP) progam. You can have your book set up and a proof copy ready to order in 24 hours, and the proof sent to you within a week. Their printing quality is as good as LSI's, and in some cases they use LSI, too.

But here is a problem with KDP: there is little to no customer support beyond email. Once they make a decision about your document files you must get them repaired or modified according to their rules or the book is not published. You may have better luck solving problems by visiting their community forum where there are many other authors who help each other answer critical questions.

KDP also have a policy which puts a floor of $10 on the amount of royalties you are paid. If you never meet that floor you will never be paid the money. Some authors have waited up to a year to get paid the smallest amount of money, and only if they have sold anything over the minimum. They also do not accept PayPal.

Due to KDP's book return policy where no books can be returned, most booksellers will not order books from them, so you are paying full price for less options than with other services. They claim you are not eligible for distribution worldwide, which is total nonsense; and they will make you use their publisher name and imprint. KDP aims to keep your book or ebook in Amazon and nowhere else.

Many people do buy their own ISBNs to establish their own publishing names or imprints as the publisher of record. If you use a *KDP* ISBN, *Amazon* is shown as the publisher, not you or your proprietary imprint. Authors have been inconvenienced by this distinction, as they are then associated with Amazon and there are many booksellers which will not work with authors who use *KDP*. To exercise all your options according to your rights as the owner of the content, I recommend using **LSI or Ingam Spark** instead.

The third on my list is **Lulu** *(www.lulu.com)*, but I have to warn you that they are less interested in being seen as a bookseller than a publishing service. They do provide the capacity to publish and print your books without set up fees or extra charges, and offer a rudimentary "marketplace" if you want to sell through your own site or through them. Their printing quality is as good as *Lightning Source,* and on occasion they will actually use LSI as their printing service. But, staff is extremely slow to respond or you get a canned response more often than not.

The equation they use to price your book depends on what you want done with it. If all you are doing is selling direct from your site or to independent bookstores, your cost is limited to the cost of printing plus shipping. If you want to sell through Lulu's marketplace they will take 20% of *net sales,* which is the retail price less their commission and cost to print.

But if you want distribution to Amazon, you will have to purchase their distribution package, naming Lulu as the publisher, and accept their retail markup. This will get you a free ISBN but your "royalty" (net revenues) will be cut in half. They also charge about 40% more than other publishing services for printing.

If you want to sell worldwide, their global distribution package includes an ISBN, which you have to pay for. Lulu also employs "packages" of services for which they will charge you more. If you are happy with that, it is still considerably more expensive than *Lightning Source* in the long run. The only real advantage to using *Lulu* is that it will accept PayPal as a payment source so you will not have to max out your credit card paying for their services.

However, here is the biggest problem with *Lulu*. If you opt to use their distribution package, the calculations they use to arrive at a reasonable *Suggested Retail Price* are ridiculously high. I will explain more about costing and pricing later. But suffice to say that, if you are keen to sell on Amazon with *Lulu*, be prepared to price yourself out of the market.

Their system of support for authors and publishers is also rather byzantine. Their Live Chat line only works certain hours of the day, and each problem is supported by a "ticket" process which only adds to the user's wait time for help, which is sometimes more than 72 hours. So expect delays in response and sometimes no help at all.

There have also been complaints about their shipping service, which appears to work on "we'll get to it when we get to it". Authors have complained about inconvenient and costly delays, missing packages; and in one case, the books were not even printed on time.

Lulu pays royalties only when they get paid for the books sold, and you are paid 30 days after the month in which the sale was made from your own storefront. For sales from Amazon, the delay in sales reporting can be as much as 90 days after the end of the month. This is not *Lulu*'s policy, it is Amazon's, and you have no control over it.

If you are only after printing one or several copies to distribute to friends, *Lulu* is the best and least troublesome option. For more information about their production specifications, see their web site.

Other self-help publishers like **AuthorHouse**, **PublishAmerica**, **iUniverse** and so on, all offer similar services which are just easy draws to authors and wouldbe publishers in search of an inexpensive way to get published, only to hook them and make them pay exhorbitant fees above their claims.

Many of these services are slow to pay an author or publisher the profit on sales, or find some excuse to charge *double* what it costs to actually print and ship the book for sale, both to you as the author/publisher and to the customer. They are in effect acting as a middle man, and you get to bear all of the costs associated with their creation of your book.

On top of that, they charge a commission for the sale of the book, reducing your profit margin even more. Some do not even offer a storefront of any kind, which means that you are stuck with the cost to print and all other costs associated with selling the book. As with

KDP, staff is extremely slow to respond. *AuthorHouse* has recently been sued for breach of contract, as has *PublishAmerica*.

I do *not* recommend **CafePress**. It lists the books for you for their base price plus your royalty, using what they call "blanks". They decide the retail price, collect the whole amount from the customer, ship it and keep 85% of the proceeds. Many authors do not see more than a few pennies for every book sold, and their retail prices are wildly out of proportion with other books of the same type. They are also quite byzantine in their category system, so expect little to no sales at all unless your book happens to be a bestseller. I guarantee it will be buried under thousands of other listings, just like on Amazon.

No doubt all of this sounds daunting to you, but I am not trying to discourage you from pursuing your dream of being published. I am warning you about what you are likely to run into because I've been there myself.

About Digital Publishing And Ebooks

This is a relatively new feature to self-publishing which is loaded with all sorts of bells, whistles, flying monkeys and other amazing and magical elements; some or all of which have nothing to do with reality on the ground.

I had already been waiting for the development of cell phones and paperless reading ever since I saw the old **STAR TREK** episode titled, *"Where No Man Has Gone Before"* in 1966, in which the concept of a library computer and the portable communicator (that cell phone you own) was introduced to the general public. Many fans of that show were called "geeks" with derogatory intent, but if it were not for them the progress of personal computers and the nifty devices which are taken for granted today would have died on the drawing board.

And, if not for the civilian arm of NASA and the space program, technology would never have been developed to enable you to microwave popcorn, let alone have all the broadband energy you need to make a video call across the world, or even GPS.

Having said that, the rapid development of file storage, sharing, image processing and all the things we use today to prepare a book for printing or display has brought us to this point. We can and do have it and eat it, too. So I must discuss the best ways to make your book accessible to millions of readers with the push of a button.

The **ebook** (or e-book) is the electronic form of your printed book presented in a digital format. Its convenience is in that it is paperless and can be read on a personal computer or laptop as well as a variety of different communication and reading devices like the iPod, the iPad, the Kindle, The Nook, and a whole list of cell phones like the BlackBerry and the Android. Now that tablet computers have come into play, one can call up any book and read it full size, including sound and the interactive feature of bookmarking with a link.

The ebook makes a wonderful marketing and selling tool for your printed book. If you want to get online reviews, offer it for a limited time for free. The more people read your ebook, the more of them will want to buy the printed book itself. Or you can produce a *preview* containing a group of sample chapters converted to an ebook for people to download and read before buying.

It is cheaper to produce than the book itself, and can be converted into a variety of formats: PDF, HTML, ePub, LIT, MOBI and so on. It can be the same size as the hard copy or made smaller to fit a smaller screen, and is more flexible than a paper book in that you can feature color images in the text and you do not need to worry about the gutter space or the size of your margins getting in the way.

There are some limitations, of course. One cannot produce and upload an ebook file greater than 100MB without special treatment, and then some email servers will not upload them without enclosing them in a compression envelope like WinZIP, Uploader, and so on. Publishers like Amazon's KDP and Barnes & Noble Press will not accept files bigger than 2MB to 5MB, so textbooks are typically not published in ebook form.

The ebook can be priced lower than a print book because there is no printing cost involved. I usually offer the full ebooks for sale for no more than $10. In all cases, the inexpensive version is made available to those with more economical minds and for travelers who cannot take the physical books with them.

If you feel it necessary, you can buy a separate ISBN for your ebook, but most people do not. The ebook is treated as a separate edition of the book, so do not list the ebook and the book as one and the same with the same ISBN. The ISBN for the printed book only pertains to it and no other version. If you are working with a service, for example, you can list your ebook with them in a selected digital format, but you have to produce an ISBN for that format. This can get pricey, so you can stay with the best standard formats possible: PDF and ePub. Anything else is worked out with the individual site hosting your ebook. Ingram Spark, for example, does not do well at selling ebooks. Amazon does. Barnes & Noble is still struggling to present a good presence for selling ebooks.

Formatting an ebook depends on which publisher you are working with. It is very important that you follow their guidelines when publishing an ebook. Most, like Smashwords, will only accept a .doc file created in **Word**. They will convert the file into an acceptable format for their readers, or for multiples styles of reader.

A side note about pricing: recently, major publishers like MacMillan and Harper Collins have raised the issue of the appropriate pricing of an ebook as the same price or only slightly less than the hardcover price. Do not make the same mistake. These publishers, only now realizing the power of reading devices like *Kindle, iPad,* and Barnes & Noble's *Nook,* have stirred up a hornet's nest with the readers using such devices.

Readers and other publishing watchers have rightly pointed out that since the ebook is technically a different product, with different format requirements and production qualities, its price should not be the same. And Amazon, having already established its maximum ebook price at $9.99, has set the tipping point for the reading buyers. Readers incensed at the idea of paying more for ebooks have said that they will not buy these publishers' books at all in the future.

Recently, a few of these major publishers have agreed on a settlement deal with the U.S. Dept. of Justice to lower the prices of their ebooks in parity with Amazon's pricing structure, and to cancel contracts with other vendors using the agency model of pricing to sell ebooks. However, this decision sets a dangerous precedent in the publishing world for the minor league players, who already recognize the marketplace conditions on the ground, and have set their own prices accordingly.

As a self-publisher I follow this rule. I have no problem selling them, and I realize more than 90% profit on the deal. I have all the software available to produce an ebook, and the actual cost to produce is negligable.

The bottom line is that the readers have an expectation of value for their shopping dollars after shelling out $$$ for an ereading device or laptop, and it is to your benefit to fall into line. I say this *only in the case of ebooks*, since they are considered add-on features for the devices. It's like buying a doll with a huge line of extra pieces, or a deck of trading cards with booster packs. And readers hungry for new literature have no patience with the games these publishers are playing. The price point is where the readers dictate the demand.

That *Amazon* is a willing participant in the agency model and instituted it sooner than the other publishers is also a problem. Since most people have heard of the retailer and seem to trust its selling programs, people are buying *Kindles*. When that many people have an expectation of low prices for high values, anyone trying to change direction in the middle of the stream will drown.

Do not fall into line with the herd of authors who, desperate to make a sale, also make the mistake of pricing their ebooks far too low to earn anything. Many are charging only 99 cents or nothing. This will not boost sales or do anything to increase the reading value of your other books. When it comes time to earn more by taking advantage of Amazon's 70% royalty level, you will have to increase your price to the floor, which is at least $2.99. Then watch sales plummet as the readers walk away.

This is not because your books are inferior to others; it is because of the perception that an ebook sold for a cheap price is a cheap ebook and of inferior quality already. Recently, I started raising my ebook prices back to my initial levels: about half the price of the printed book. Others have done the same and are enjoying more sales as a result. The best rule of thumb is to price the ebook as high as you think is **fair**, then adjust downward. Demand rules price, not the other way around.

Amazon is a strange duck. It insists on undercutting everyone else for pricing, and discounts heavily below cost. It also practices the destructive policy of price matching, where if a competitor lowers the price of a book or ebook, Amazon will too; robbing the author or publisher of any "royalty" earned on the sale. Amazon also engages in what it calls "Daily Deals" in which it will give thousands of copies of a title away during a 24 hour period, without compensation to the author or publisher. In this way it is slowly destroying the trust it had earned with authors and publishers in the past, turning itself into a pariah in the book world. What started out as a convenient way to buy books for customers has turned into a giant black hole full of titles which will never be noticed among the ones which Amazon has published itself.

Worse, no bookseller will buy wholesale books from Amazon. The shareholders are beginning to notice that its business model does not give them any benefits, and more and more authors are starting to shy away rather than look to it for sales.

In fact, authors are realizing less sales than ever as a series of glitches in Amazon's servers in the last three years have proven to have lost sales data. These glitches are a result of frequent hacking and server attacks made by members of groups dedicated to using guerilla tactics to make their point to the giant retailer, which is slow to see anything not firmly anchored to its deck.

Here I will discuss the various types of ereader manufacturers and their products:

Amazon Kindle: As with many developments in the digital age, the *Kindle* ereader is a viable platform to present your book to people who own it, even if you do not have a print version to sell. The reason it is so popular is because it is a dedicated device. It performs one function, which is to store and display ebooks for readers who do not want to haul their library around with them wherever they go. With a 6" x 9" screen or smaller, and scroll and bookmark capability, *Kindle* owners can store as many as a thousand books in its memory for quick access.

It is also quite pricey. The device itself retails for around $139, and the ebooks associated with it run the gamut in price, from $1.99 up to $9.99. Recently, the advent of the Kindle Fire and tablet devices have set up some stiff competition with the full featured iPad, produced by Apple.

The problem with the older models was that they were not set up to project color images on their screens. Content uploaded in color was displayed as black & white or grayscale images. A lot of readers liked to read the books in the dark and could not because the Kindle did not have a backlit display screen. Now they must upgrade to the Kindle Fire to achieve their desires, and that becomes another investment of money. It is no wonder that Fire sales have never risen to their potential level. Kindle readers have also migrated over to iPad instead of buying an upgrade precisely because of this problem.

Another problem lies with the Kindle purchase agreement, which actually turns out to be a leasing agreement; where Kindle owners could "purchase" an ebook and store it on the device, but Amazon still owns the book and can and does withdraw it without notice and without refunding the money.

In 2009, Amazon was sued by a student who claimed that his copy of *1984* was withdrawn because it came from a pirated source, and the file included all his margin notes for a paper he was preparing for a class. To settle the suit Amazon offered a refund for the withdrawn book and said it would never do it again.

Later, it withdrew an entire collection of books from a customer for a "violation" of its service contract without specifying what the violation was. These kinds of actions have earned it a bad reputation among many customers.

Until recently, Amazon's *Kindle Direct Publishing* (KDP) service could only accept document files already formatted for HTML, or "Hyper Text Markup Language", which included the need to upload all the images separately in a compressed file folder. This has caused many problems for authors not familiar with HTML and the conversion processor provided by KDP. It also took as many as 12 to 72 hours for a book to go online once the files were uploaded. People were never satisfied with the results, including me, and I am the nice one.

With the debut of the Kindle 2, however, the processing of files speeded up and improved a bit, and even newer features of the *Word* processing software has made it even easier to prepare a document file for submission. KDP has also begun accepting ePub files as well as PDF files for conversion to the right format. This is especially good for books which have no illustrations.

Now, one can just upload a specially prepared Word file which they will convert to their proprietary format. However, you have to be careful with these, as there is no guarantee that people will actually read them. At the end of the day one must conclude that your files may not be getting out there and they are not going to tell you about it.

Smashwords: (*www.smashwords.com*) used to distribute ebooks for publishers and small presses to stores and online retailers at the wholesale level. They had since opened their conversion and distribution process to authors and small presses at the retail level. They distribute to a variety of online retailers.

Warning: Should you choose to use Smashwords your best option is to create a "free flow" document as a raw file, since the presence of tabs, paragraph breaks and other features of a *.doc* file appears to upset their converter. They prefer you upload a *.doc* 97-2003 file to them set up in only the most primitive formatting style, which does not include fancy fonts, tabs, tables or anything else. It must be essentially a text only file in 12 point Times Roman. They also cannot accept files larger than 7.5MB so large textbooks, children's books and anything heavily illustrated will not go up.

Also expect to get your submission rejected for formatting errors *even if* you follow their *Smashwords Style Guide*, which will tell you everything you need to do with your content. If you don't follow the guide, your ebook will be kicked back to you for correction.

The other problem you might encounter is with reporting and payment. Despite their standard service contract stating that royalties for distributions would be paid in 30 days following the month in which the sale was made, many people have been forced to wait as long as a year to get paid for sales which were made on retail sites. Smashwords can only report and pay what it gets from the retailers.

They are good about reporting the sales first, and payment is made each quarter, not monthly. But they must *wait* on the retailers to report the sales, which means there is a lot of *waiting* all around. This is something Smashwords has no control over.

Since the bulk of ebooks populating Smashwords are free or less than $1.99, there is no incentive to sell them there. Distribution is still the best option and source of sales, but it is still no guarantee that your ebook *will* sell.

Each upload must be reviewed each time for each particular market, and if you are already working with KDP or another publisher there is no need to use Smashwords to distribute to Amazon. In fact, recent events have shown that Amazon is not in any hurry to deal with Smashwords, so the distribution option is usually "no".

Smashwords does like to attach a free ISBN to any ebook destined to be shipped to sellers requiring an ISBN. This ISBN cannot be used anywhere else, so don't think to spread it across all your sellers. It is only for Smashwords editions.

Smashwords had reached a deal with several library associations where ebooks are made available for lending to library patrons. You could set up a 2-tier pricing schedule where you ask for one price to regular customers and another to the libraries.

But I have since opted to close my Smashwords account and look for another distributor because of the many difficulties cropping up with file preparation to review for actual distribution. Each step represented a substantial delay getting the book to market, and some retailers were slow to accept them if at all.

I studied what was happening and reached the conclusion that Smashwords was no longer keeping up with the latest improvements in ebook conversion, and sales had already slowed down to almost a complete stop. At some point you may come to the same decision point with your distributor. The only real solution is to move on.

Bookbaby: a "professional" conversion company which converts .docx files into epubs. I tried them out for several months. First, a file will be converted for upwards of $250. Second, their distribution platform is limited; which means that sales will be limited. They do not distribute to everyone. And, in order to recoup one's investment, one must post the ebooks on their catalog for prices which are higher than desired. I found them ineffective and moved on.

Draft2Digital: (*www.draft2digital.com*) This is a relatively new file processing service I tried out for a few months. They will accept a .docx file for conversion once it has been set up according to their guidelines. You get to see the published result before it is placed on the selling platform. You also get free distribution to various aggregators like Kobo, Barnes & Noble, and others. I published several fiction books, then some nonfiction books. But my nonfiction books were rejected because they contained content the aggregators deemed "public domain". First of all, I don't publish public domain material, and second, I wrote every word in the manuscript. But again as I said before, some will not accept nonfiction books. I may return to D2D for the fiction alone, because they do try.

Mobipocket: (*www.mobipocket.com*) This used to be operated by an individual entrepreneur out of France but has since been bought by Amazon. They provided ebooks in digital format for download primarily to Kindle. The payout is also much slower than KDP. Whereas KDP will pay you net royalties in two months, Mobipocket pays you in six. Since Kobo has begun work on its own reader, the .mobi file format has become largely superfluous.

Scribd: (*www.scribd.com*) owned and operated by Scribd, Inc. as a content management and file download platform consisting of web sites, services, software applications and networks that allows for the authorized download and distribution of written digital content over the internet.

They publish specially formatted files for reading on a variety of different devices, so you have to reformat your book files to fit their publishing engine. Their guide states that your beautifully fomatted book must be reduced to a text or RTF file before uploading as a .doc (not .docx), but a PDF will suffice. They do give you a complete instruction guide for this, as opposed to a series of formatting instructions from separate modules.

They also operate a store where you can sell your ebook. But be warned: *Scribd* **is not very good at selling ebooks**. They are more geared toward free downloads and sampling, and if you are not careful you can end up giving your ebooks away because free ebooks are the only items being read.

Further, evidence of piracy has surfaced where pirate publishers have begin uploading illegally obtained content from Scribd for sale or free giveaways on their own sites. The FBI Internet Crime division cannot keep up with the flow.

Also, Scribd has recently changed its hosting format to a subscription service, where for a low fee the customer can download and read any book available. If you are thinking of using Scribd, I would remind you that this means a long wait for any money from sales.

Lulu (*www.lulu.com*) has also entered the ebook publishing world by enabling people to upload files for conversion to PDFs and ePubs. Their cost to publish is currently 99¢ plus 20% commission. For $99 they will also convert your ebook to an ePub file compatible with Apple for their iBookstore.

But be warned: Apple has the final say as to whether your book will be accepted *even after* you have paid for this service. They have some rather limiting and rigid requirements about the subject matter as well as the layout and formatting. They also require an ISBN for your ebook, and you *will* have to accept Lulu as the publisher of your book or not at all.

Kobo (*www.kobo.ca*) has a similar requirement, and you must go through the same problems as with Smashwords since they only accept raw or epub files. They are also based in Canada so if you are in the U. S. there is also a risk of high tariffs and VAT (value added tax) being attached to the retail price. So I would not go there either.

The best option for the budding ebook publisher: *do it yourself*.

I recommend **Calibre** (*www.kovidgoyal.net/calibre*), a file processing application which can be downloaded to your own computer. It is available for both PC and MAC and offered as a free download but please, be nice and donate something to the cause. The developer is a California based programmer who has created a good alternative to going through a third party for conversion. The latest version takes care of its own download and installation into your C:// drive, and maintains your elibrary for you.

With calibre you can generate your own **.epub, PDF, lit, mobi,** and other types of files for uploading to any market you choose, or for loading into your own device. It will also generate *.opf* files for previews, though I prefer creating PDFs, as *opfs* are specially encrypted and may not be readable on some computers.

To create a source file for this engine, I recommend that you create a **.docx** file. Calibre will then convert the file to a version of your choice. There are several improvements which include filling out a metadata description form and a cover uploader, plus new features which allow you to format the raw file so that it will convert cleanly. Be sure to pass the finished product through *epubchecker* to make sure it is readable.

You can also download the files to disk and store them on your personal computer for uploading to whichever publishing service you choose. This is especially useful for devices which will only read .*epub*s. And there you have it.

With the debut of the Kindle, the Kindle 2, Nook, the Surface and "digital paper", one would think that the future of traditional print publishing looks pretty bleak. Yet, for all the doom and gloom over paper books and the closure of bookstores which had stood the test of time through as many as three wars, there will always be room for printed books.

In fact, the statistics show that only about 25% of all books sold are ebooks. I read comments from readers to this day that they will never abandon printed books, and there is news that more readers are flocking to bookstores instead of shopping online.

The other difficulty with losing printed books altogether is that some books will never convert properly without paying an exhorbitant sum to do it. Children's picture books, photography and art books, and textbooks with numerous graphs and illustrations, all demand special treatment or a great deal of time to convert properly. Thus, the print book will never go away in our lifetime.

I see digital books as an adjunct to the printed word and a convenience to the busy reader who is always on the go, or a way to store older books for restoration later. Digital publishing will never replace the lovely feel of a page full of ink words and pictures for those who treasure the process. And books will ever be part of the antiquarian's collection, especially those which cannot be easily produced in ebook format.

But as the economy continues to adjust to continuing pressures on it, publishers find themselves squeezed by market forces and the need to economize. The only winners in this particular market will be those who adapt their business models to the new economy, spend less and increase their output.

As a self-publisher you need to examine your methods and solutions every step of the way, because what you spend to make your books attractive to buyers can add up more rapidly than you realize.

Digital piracy. A new problem which has sprung up in the last ten years, and which can affect your profits in a significant way. There are those who use the internet just the same way you do, but with larceny on their minds. It's no surprise that a flood of black market and bootlegged goods in the digital marketplace is on the rise. Cheap knockoffs are part and parcel of the growing trade imbalance with other countries, coupled with the greed of persons who enjoy their success on the backs of hard working creative folks.

Digital pirates are everywhere, and they will try to take anyone's work and make money from their sale without recompense to the creator. Digital pirates can also be those who feel that if they do not have the money to pay for it they can just take it. Sorry, but that's just not jake. The department stores do not give things away for free. A grocery store does not give away food for free. A digital or print book is a commodity just like the clothes on your back and the shoes you wear. You paid for *them*, didn't you?

The issue arises from some years back when file sharing sites like Napster and others of its ilk began ripping off music and videos and started sharing the files with hundreds of users for free.

Later, Chinese-made goods like pirated CDs and books began appearing on eBay with penny minimum bids. Those sellers never delivered the goods they were paid for. The practical effect was that many legitimate traders left eBay for good, declaring that as long as this was going on no one could make any money; especially when eBay charged higher listing fees and settlement fees than they do now. eBay has since lowered its listing fees for books but unless you are confident of a huge interest in your item the listing will expire with no bid at all more often than not. This is how eBay makes most of its survival money. It is not interested in you as a vendor. It is only interested in earning fees from transactions.

Digital piracy also occurs when one CD, DVD or audio book is reproduced thousands of times over for sale by sellers who stand on street corners, or when they are offered online for sale for ten times their actual price.

One of the many reasons your purchased CD will not play in certain modes is that the data has been encrypted or sealed in, often with software which you do not have easy access to. If you want to manipulate the track or video in any way you have to have a user id and the password to access it. Some devices will not play these discs at all if they have no software which can interpolate the data and "release" it for playing.

The result is that you are forced to buy the latest hardware in order to play it, which then adds to the price of the enjoyment of your music or movie. At some point the law of diminishing returns will kick in.

It is the ease and convenience of using the internet which can be blamed for the prevalence of digital piracy, but ultimately the pirates will be located and shut down for the mere fact that they chose an extremely public venue from which to ply their trade. Their IP addresses can be traced, and as more customers get burned, sites like *Ripoff Report* will proclaim their piracy to anyone who wants to know.

The way to avoid such piracy is to avoid sharing your creative spirit with sites which publish ebooks and articles *exclusively for free* instead of for sale. Digital pirates mine these sites constantly for the materials they need. You should not be giving *anything* away if you want to make any money for your work, and your file sharing should extend only to the previews you post to encourage people to buy. Give them three chapters at most, and let them pay for the rest. In this way you thwart those who want to make money off your own hard work.

Here is a nifty way I create galley files to prepare my ebooks for sale from secure market sites. They prevent easy print offs, and no one can create a book from them easily without having to do the whole thing over.

I take the book's interior and strip out all the formatting for printing. I reduce the margins to .1 or .2 inches all around. I make the total flow of the file "continuous" and remove the headers and footers. I set the page size to 6" x 9" (a custom printing size), remove the gutter and "mirror margins" and set it to "normal". I also remove all the section and page breaks, except where it is practical. When I save the document I save it in "print view". Then I create a PDF of the document. If I want to create a preview of the book I just truncate the file past a certain point. This makes the file uniform and unprintable. No watermarks are necessary.

But all of the above is useless if you do not do everything to call attention to your book.

You're Published! Now What?

Distributors, Affiliates and Selling Partners

It is up to your printer to provide you with information about distributors and other resources. If they do not, there are many articles and listings on *Google* which will help you to obtain one. Here are some definitions to help you:

A distributor is a central or regional supplier of books from a variety of different sources to both wholesalers and retailers. A distributor is not legally necessary to sell your books. You can still sell them directly in whatever quantity you want to from your own store or web site, but if you are ambitious enough to reach out to the major booksellers, a distributor is an important part of your selling program.

Ingram Book Group is the largest and best distribution source on the planet, but they ask for a catalog of at least ten books on tap before they will carry you. If you do not have enough books to fill that requirement but are determined to start your own publishing business, I recommend *Ingram Spark* for a fully professional printing source which uses Ingram's distribution channel, listing *Amazon, Barnes & Noble, Powell's Books*, and a whole cadre of other book listing sites online which they supply with print on demand books as well as books produced by the traditional offset printing process.

You pay a small fee per year to list your book on their catalog, and their bookselling partners will order books based on their customer demands.

Baker & Taylor was once a formidable distribution source with regional shipping warehouses which made it easier to get your book into the stores. They relied on *Lightning Source* for some of their catalog listings. Recently, Baker & Taylor "retired" from book distribution and has partnered with several other aggregators to produce and sell books. But their publishing arm only caters to large publishers.

Companies like **Amazon, Barnes & Noble, Powell's Books, Target**, and **Buy.com** will list your books for sale once they receive the title through the distributor's catalog offerings. I have had my books listed on several hundred bookselling sites all over the world as a result of working with *Ingram Spark* (LSI). If you feel you can handle the extra work you can try to approach them yourself but I would recommend getting a single source of distribution.

But remember that having your book listed is no guarantee of sales; only the ease and convenience of selling books through them. *You still have to do something to promote and sell the books yourself.* Do not expect to list your books and then sit back and wait for the money to pour in because it will not. Only your proactive approach to marketing and selling your own work will get the results you want. And remember that your book is competing for attention with *millions* of others all over the world. Your book is but one needle in a very large haystack.

When you are using *Lulu* or one of the other publishing services, you can use their distribution channels to list your books; but since **they do not allow returns** for wholesale orders, you will not have a snowball's chance that your books will be picked up by the major booksellers, except possibly Amazon.

More about this in the next section, ***Copyrights And Content Control***.

An **affiliate** is a loose term for a subsidiary or registered bookseller associated with a specific shopping site, like **Amazon** or **eBay**. If you look at book reviewer sites or reading sites online you may find that many are powered directly or indirectly by Amazon. If you add your book listing to them they may try to restrict you to the Amazon listings alone, but that should not stop you from exploring your options. You can also become an affiliate on their sites by listing books from their inventory on your own site, then earn a commission from their sales.

Be warned that becoming an *Amazon* affiliate is a risky proposition, especially if you happen to be based in a state which is in contention with Amazon for the collection of sales tax. Amazon *can and does drop affiliations* if they have to collect the tax in that state. To date they have discontinued affiliations in 10 states so far, and I do not know how much money has been paid out or withheld from the affiliates, since Amazon is notorious for not reporting numbers.

eBay is rapidly becoming a logistical nightmare in terms of affiliations and their selling program changes every week. In fact, the number of complaints about eBay would fill a book. eBay's changes in order to become more like Amazon have generated complaints and even a lawsuit over the sales and shipment of products.

I would not enroll in either, unless your sole source of income is from them. In that case, you need to find a way to sell on your own and fulfill on your own. That is what your own web site is for. I strongly suggest that you establish one and market your book from its pages alone. The benefits of remaining independent is worth gold in this business.

A selling partner is a bookseller or other product company to which you can submit your book for sale as part of a product package, a service, or part of a relatable *genre**. For example, a publisher with several different products in the gaming industry can partner with a book publisher which has several titles in the same or relatable genre, and in that way share the costs of sales and the profits generated therefrom. In fact, I participated in such a partnership several years ago. The partnership only dissolved when the hosting site went down and my partner established her own site.

In addition to providing free publicity and promotion for each other, the word will spread that you are established as an author and publisher in the genre you want to approach. Viral publicity like this is a very valuable part of your marketing program, which I will discuss in a later section. *A genre is a specific subject of interest, such as literature, fiction, nonfiction, adventure, mystery, westerns, history, science fiction, fantasy, comics, philosophy, romance, and so on; and their subgenres.

Copyrights And Content Control

The standard rule of thumb is that once you have written and published a story it is copyrighted. You place the copyright information on the second inside page (the *copyright page*) after the title page. A copyright for a book remains in effect until 70 years after the author's death and can be extended by the author's estate in virtual perpetuity. No one may copy your book word for word, nor sell derivative or edited versions of your book containing significant portions of your book, without your legal permission. For more information about copyrights and the legal issues arising from them, look to *www.copyright.gov*.

As I discussed before, you can also repackage a book in public domain for sale under your own imprint but you should do a title search before you do. Often the estate or the descendents of an author may own the *proprietary* rights as well as the copyrights for the work and if you publish it in its entirety without their permission they have the right to sue.

Also, many antiquarian book collectors may become offended if you attempt to reprint a book whole in its original format. They feel that you are destroying the "uniqueness" of the book. Before you proceed with publishing a book in the public domain make sure it is an *"orphan"* work first.

For example, let me cite the ongoing problem with **Google**: the popular search engine and web hosting site has been charged with violating copyrights when it comes to listing books in its ever expanding network library. Its founders entered into a difficult and contentious situation when they decided to start offering books out of print and in public domain on the site as part of the project. While its goal is laudible, its method is draconian.

Lawsuits aimed at restoring the rights to collect royalties from the sale of most of the books they scanned pointed out the problem in detail. Google did not once inquire as to the copyright status of the books, relying on free sharing sites like *Gütenberg.org* for its direction and as a model for free book sharing. Many authors will point out that free book sharing sites are the reason they are not selling books.

The Authors Guild and the Science Fiction Writers of America have questioned the legal validity of Google's selling program and took it to court.

In 2008, Google offered a settlement to the suitors which did not cover all the affected books, and left out an entire library of books from Europe. While the courts argued through the issue, Google continued to scan and list the books it selected without any pause to date.

In 2010 a federal district court ruled that the settlement was illegal and that Google could no longer scan books without permission. To follow up, members of a French consortium of publishers brought suit against Google to collect back royalties due to their authors.

In 2013 a circuit court ruled that there was no merit to the suits brought, citing a suit against Apple and six major publishing houses which challenged their right to maintain high prices for ebooks. While it looks like apples and oranges, the judge stated that the benefit to the consumer of offering free content and lower prices for ebooks outweighed the copyrights of the content owners.

73

So now, less and less authors are taking "advantage" of its book search program and would rather not deal with the giant at all. I have also refrained as I did not see any sales benefit from posting the books in a place where customers could read the entire book without paying for it first. This "freedom" of search is at the crux of the violation of copyright law, which is clearly set.

There is also the question of whether it is truly creative content if you are forced to publish old books by other authors in order to pad your book list. Very often, a self-publisher can start with one original book and do better than with a whole raft of reprints.

You can opt to sell a publisher certain rights to issue your book in a given territory, like First North American Publication Rights, which grants the publisher permission to print and distribute the book only in North America (the United States, Canada, and Mexico). The publisher must pay you for the rights for each territory they feel your books will sell in. However, some publishers have been said to buy the rights for one region and then issue the book in all the territories they cover. This is unethical, but sadly the norm.

These publishers will also claim a *proprietary* **right** to publishing and distribution of your work and treat you the author as an independent contractor, entitled only to the minimum amount of compensation enforceable by law. By *proprietary* that means that they consider your work their private property. That is why it is vitally important for you to do your homework before you accept their terms or sign on the dotted line.

Usually the rights are spelled out in the **contract**, which is *a legally binding document that can be modified or amended only by mutual consent.* If they are not, you need to go back and ask for one, or read the one you have agreed to so that you know exactly what they want and what benefits they are willing to give you. If there is something in the contract which you do not understand or agree with, ask questions. It is essential that you know what you are guaranteed and what you must give up going in, or you will lose out on all the rights and benefits as well as monetary compensation you are rightfully owed.

The watchword here is: **trust but verify**. Do not just sign the document without reading it over very carefully, because a contract can become a velvet trap.

For example, I was contacted recently by Nook Press, the publishing arm for the Nook device which was the ebook publisher for Barnes & Noble. Before this, my ebooks were published by PubIt, which was taken over by Nook Press. When I read the new contract, I saw immediately that there were flaws in the language; giving no consideration whatsoever to the content provider (me) and reserving the right to modify or terminate the agreement at any time and without any reason "at our discretion".

This is an example of what I call a "shadow" contract. It would not be a binding agreement, it is easily rendered null and void in civil court, and the author or publisher is left entirely out of the decision making process. They asked me to publish nicely twice after I pulled my titles from PubIt; and each time I said, "thanks, but no thanks."

Later, in 2018 I published a few books under their aegis and found the project fruitless. I have never sold any books through Nook Press, which has been renamed "Barnes & Noble Press", but it is no different or operated than the former. Still later, I read that Barnes & Noble was sold to hedge fund operator Elliott Advisors, headed by Paul Singer, for $638 million. In the meantime, their Press is in limbo.

If you have the money to invest, retain a lawyer which specializes in copyright and contract law so that he can iron this out for you. A lawyer will help you to read between the lines for your legal and emotional well being. Get all your answers before you sign at the bottom line, because once you do you are stuck.

I have heard of publishers selling the rights for a book to a studio for movie production without consulting with the owner of the copyright or the author first. In each case, the creator is entitled to compensation in the form of a cash outlay or a percentage of the gross ticket sales, and may have to fight in court for it. Lawsuits of this kind have delayed the start of a production or shelved it outright because someone did not read the contract clearly, or took liberties with the property at issue.

Often it is not the publishing company at fault for this particular blunder but an ambitious or unscrupulous production or publishing executive. This is why the contract is the most important instrument for your protection.

I had one such experience myself when I happened to be walking across a hotel lobby and found myself near a movie set. The production posted a sign on a sandwich board proclaiming the title. Curious, I asked one of the crew what the movie was about. To my surprise I found out that someone wrote a screenplay about a treasure hunt. When I went home and told my friends about it, a legal search brought up the issue of copyright infringement between my friends, who were the original creators of the hunt game, and the producers of the film. The producers settled out of court.

If a legal dispute arises with regard to **plagiarism** (copying or quoting another author word for word) or a territory or ownership conflict, you can and should submit your book to the copyright office in your country to register it, thereby sealing your ownership of the book as well as its content. Very often the copyright is not questioned if you simply declare it on the copyright page, so there is no need for urgency, but if you are concerned about such issues do register it by all means. It is better to invest the extra expense if you want to cover all the bases. If, however, the other author claims what is called "coincident design", you must share the credit or blame for any confusion on the part of the readers.

Another word about plagiarism: I have been participating on a forum for authors in which one of the members has freely admitted that he changed the title of one of his books and reworked the cover to closely resemble another, in order to "gain a market advantage" over the other author. But this particular member claimed that he was a lawyer as well. On further questioning, he admitted to have gotten a degree from a well known institution of law. This did not exonerate him from the illegality of his plagiarist practices.

Lo and behold, the very next day this same university announced that it was *expelling* a group of students for cheating, from exam copying to buying professional papers and putting their names on the front pages instead of writing the papers themselves. Obviously, the author of the post did not see how much damage he could do to his own reputation; not to mention the school which awarded him a diploma. If that was at all true. At that point I was extremely skeptical of his claim.

Another had come out and said that he copy-pasted another author's work, then published it under his own name.

Both authors could not see that these tactics were harming anyone. When it was pointed out to them through a flood of responses from all quarters that it was plagiarism and misleading to readers to engage in these methods in order to gain a fair market advantage, they were entirely unapologetic.

It is not only unethical to plagiarize, it is just plain cheating, not to mention in clearly bad taste, to copy from another's work word for word, or in any other way to render one's own work *indistinguishable* from another. Not only does it make you a pariah in the book world, no major publisher will pick your book to publish if there is any evidence that you plagiarized the book in question.

Amazon has chosen to block both these authors from selling their books. One of them has had his account closed altogether. They are incensed about this, but I have only one good thing to say about Amazon: they know when something is a bad move.

Amazon is a business, and whenever something occurs which puts its business in jeopardy, it will act aggressively in whatever manner is legally open to it. Sometimes you have to be cruel to be kind.

Content control. This is a sticky wicket indeed. When you set up a book with a self-help printing service, the agreement is usually posted online for you to read and examine. Some of them will not let you submit your files until you have put a check in their little agreement box saying that you have read and agreed to it. The caveat is that *once you submit the files for printing you have agreed to the contract as it stands*.

Be careful with this. Some of these publishers can and do change the member agreement, contract and/or policies in their favor, sometimes **without notice** and at their own discretion, like with Nook Press. Frequently, you have no say in this if you still want to work with them. If you have an issue as an individual author or publisher, their usual response is that if you do not like it you can go elsewhere.

I agree. *You should never feel like you are trapped in a bargain which is one-sided or offers no consideration for your rights as the creator and owner of the content.* You *are* better off going elsewhere, and they will be losing all the fruits of your hard work, not to mention damaging their reputation as an honest company in the publishing world. With such an image poisoning the deal, most authors learn to avoid a similar situation, and it is incumbent on the publisher to change its business practices to mitigate any liability for a lengthy lawsuit.

If you are not sure about using a specific publishing service, just look at their community forums, where you can find praise as well as complaints about its policies and performance. Do a comparison of the printing costs and the way they approach distribution among all the publishers you are interested in. You can even do a search of consumer complaint sites to determine how much risk your investment will incur in participation with the self-help service you choose.

A secondary consideration to content control is the issue of selling and pricing. This also includes the right to compete in the open marketplace unfettered by the overarching interference of the major marketing sites. Amazon, Barnes & Noble, Smashwords, or any site which sells books and ebooks should not be in the business of picking and choosing authors or publishers. They are in the business of selling, which means you have the right to refuse their services.

As a self-publisher, I do not sell through any of them. I sell direct from my own site, set up to sell only my content. In this highly competitive universe, you can establish yourself better by selling direct and giving those stores, *which are also your competitors*, a wide berth. You would collect more revenues, and there would be a wider market to reach.

Amazon is successful because it has locked in the content to be read only on its devices, by readers who chose to buy them only through its storefront. But it cannot prevent you from selling your own content yourself. It crows to all and sundry that it is the only place to shop, but there is a growing number of publishers like myself who are not buying the hype and choosing to remain independent. The corporation is trying to establish a monopoly, but has failed because of the growth of competitors like Apple, Google, Kobo and others.

This brings up the issue of monopoly and also violations of antitrust laws.

What Are The Antitrust Laws?

They are a system of state and federal laws that prohibit unwarranted restraints on free and open competition. They allow the Attorney General of any state to bring civil and criminal legal actions against individuals and businesses acting in restraint of trade. District attorneys can bring similar actions for antitrust offenses centered in their counties. The law provides that anyone injured by an antitrust offense may recover from the wrongdoer up to 3 times the damages suffered.

As a consumer or taxpayer antitrust offenses almost always raise the prices paid by consumers. Being forced to pay illegally high prices is the equivalent of having money stolen from your pocket. Even relatively small price increases can have a tremendous effect. Also, lowering the price to a dangerously low level can cause similar harm. Consumers suffer from the economic dislocations caused by these antitrust offenses.

As an owner of a business the cost of doing business affects the profit a business will make. If the price of goods or services used by your business is raised by antitrust restraints, your cost of doing business will rise. Some antitrust offenses can make it impossible for you to do any business.

I can't give a complete list and description of possible antitrust offenses here. However, the following will identify the most important activities you should be aware of.

Horizontal price-fixing - It is illegal for any competitors to have an agreement to raise, stabilize or otherwise affect prices. The agreement does not have to be in writing or otherwise formalized. Even an informal understanding concerning prices between competitors is illegal. The agreement does not have to set specific prices. Any agreement affecting price levels is illegal. Even a practice of exchanging price information with competitors, where this practice affects prices, violates the antitrust laws.

For example: in 2011, the United States Department of Justice filed suit against Apple and five other major publishing companies, charging that they colluded with each other to raise their ebook prices to as much as $15.99; and to switch from the wholesale pricing model to what is called the "agency" model, where the publisher, not the retailer, sets the price.

No one in the publishing community could hardly fathom what this meant to smaller companies in competition with both Amazon and the giants. Amazon had already switched to the agency model on its own, but set a ceiling of $9.99 for ebook prices across the board. Ebooks set above that level were heavily discounted and the publishers were naturally concerned about their profit margins.

Several of the accused publishers withdrew their printed books from the Amazon catalog as a result, saying that the price was far below their cost to produce the content. But Amazon was somehow exempt from any prosecution by the Dept. of Justice for price-fixing on its own, discounting ebook prices often below their cost to publish.

The court entertained papers and amicus briefs defending the publishers from bookseller and writing associations alike. Each blamed Amazon for setting the precedent and suggested that it was more guilty than the accused publishers.

Eventually, a settlement was achieved which called for the affected publishers to terminate their contracts with Apple and any other retailer which engaged with them under the agency pricing model, and they were ordered to pay a fine for collusion.

As to whether they will continue to supply ebooks to Amazon is another matter. The settlement has encouraged the giant retailer to violate the unspoken rules. It has not only fixed prices on its catalog, it has price matched with other retailers in competition with it, often undercutting them in price and driving prices below a reasonable or profitable level. It affects both independent authors and small presses, with the result that many are forced to capitulate to the monopsony Amazon has created for itself.

Lucky for us there are now enough competitors to prevent Amazon from gaining an unfair advantage, but the flood of hopefuls falsely convinced that Amazon has their good in mind continues unabated.

Other agreements among competitors - In addition to price-fixing, any other agreement among competitors which restrains competition is usually illegal. For example, *boycotts,* agreements by competitors not to sell to particular customers or not to buy from particular suppliers; *market or customer allocations*, agreements among competitors affecting to whom or where each will sell; and *output limitations,* agreements among competitors to limit the overall quantities to be marketed, are almost always illegal regardless of justification.

Joint ventures undertaken by mutual competitors can be legal within certain limits. So far, we see that even competitors agree that a tolerable level of risk is involved when deciding not to supply, but I have not seen competitors openly agree to do anything like that.

As for Amazon, it remains closed mouthed about its own business model, which claims to be farsighted but is actually quite myopic about the facts on the ground. There have been calls for Amazon to be broken up because many businesses have been priced out of the market altogether.

Vertical price-fixing (resale price maintenance) - Any agreement between a seller and a buyer regarding the price at which the buyer *resells* a product is illegal. Any attempt by a seller to have a buyer enter into such an agreement is also illegal.

Example: A manufacturer of light bulbs complains to a hardware store because the store is selling bulbs below the suggested retail price. The store promises that it will in the future keep its light bulb price within 10 percent of the suggested retail price. The manufacturer and the store are engaged in vertical price-fixing. This has worked in reverse with Amazon, which decides at what price it will sell the product. This is legal, but is it ethical to sell below margin?

Other agreements between sellers and buyers - While agreements between a buyer and a seller that affect prices are always illegal, agreements that *restrict* the buyer's freedom to resell products can also be illegal. These agreements include restrictions on where and to whom the buyer may resell the product. Such restraints are illegal whenever they harm competition more than they help it.

Example: A publisher discovers that two of its wholesale distributors are trying to sell its books to the same store and that they are offering discounts in order to make the sale. The publisher forbids one of the wholesalers to sell to the store. The publisher has placed a customer restriction on the wholesaler.

This is why it is often advisable to rely only on one distributor to make the sale. Not only are they in competition, they can also restrict the content in such a way as to make it unmarketable. In general it is wise policy to accept the lower bid, but the actual supplier is left out of the loop.

Tying - Sellers sometimes require a buyer to purchase a product the buyer does not want in order to be allowed to buy a product the buyer does want. Such requirements are called tying arrangements. Tying is generally illegal where *the seller has some degree of control over the market for the product the buyer wants.*

Example: A wholesale book distributor is the only company distributing a best selling book in the city, but it requires bookstores to buy a certain number of less popular books if they want the best seller. The distributor is imposing a tying arrangement.

A similar situation was illustrated in the antitrust lawsuit between Booklocker.com and Amazon. In late March of 2008 the news broke that Amazon had begun a new policy requiring print on demand (POD) publishers using Amazon's distribution services to print their books using only Amazon's subsidiaries *BookSurge* and *Createspace*.

This led Booklocker.com, an independent POD publisher, to initiate a class action antitrust lawsuit challenging the legality of this policy. The lawsuit claimed that Amazon was illegally tying the *BookSurge* printing service to Amazon's distribution services. The SPAN (Small Publishers Association of North America) Board voted to support the class action suit. So did the Authors Guild of America.

During 2008, the outcry expanded to *Lulu*, a publishing house which I had used, and for a while there was a question of whether *Lulu* would be forced to use *BookSurge* in order to distribute books to Amazon. Since then, *Lulu* not only knuckled under, the outrageous difference between the prices I had set for my books and the prices which they would have sold for forced me to make some critical decisions; one of which was to avoid buying distribution services through Lulu altogether. Today I have not regretted my decision.

Toward the end of 2009, Amazon quietly merged *BookSurge* with *CreateSpace,* effectively ending the situation with Booklocker.com. It is also possible that this was just another tactic to avoid prosecution for antitrust violation. After all, if the publisher is someone else, then the problem no longer exists, does it?

In 2010 Booklocker.com and Amazon reached a settlement which actually relieved Amazon of the task of facing a jury. What Amazon does in 2019 will determine whether it will violate any more rules. Thus far, my own experience with *CreateSpace* in 2012 made me contemplate filing a suit of my own. The better option was to move to *Lightning Source* instead, and wash my hands of the problem altogether. This saved me money which would have been wasted on legal fees against an unmitigated monster with unlimited resources.

Note that in 2018, *CreateSpace* was absorbed by KDP.

Monopoly - *A business may not unfairly keep others from competing with it.* Businesses may and should compete to obtain customers, and growth through superior ability and efficiency is not illegal. However, a business with significant market power may not take actions that exclude or handicap its competitors. In the case of Amazon, they cannot prevent me from selling my own books. But their competitive tactics do much to make life difficult for a small publisher like me. Undercutting competitors on price to drive sales, or using the ebooks as loss leaders to sell their Kindles, makes Amazon a jaguar in the jungle of retailers.

Mergers - *Businesses may not merge with or acquire other businesses, when the effect may be substantially lessen competition.* The purpose of this federal statute is to stop the anticompetitive effects of increasing concentration or market power at an early stage. Such mergers and acquisitions may result in higher prices for consumers and other buyers. Mergers between competitors are more likely to raise concerns, but mergers between companies in other relationships, such as supplier and customer, may also be illegal.

While Amazon's CEO Jeff Bezos makes the claim that he is only striving to bring the best products everywhere to its customers, the way in which he chooses to do this is dubious. By buying out smaller retailers and publishing services, Amazon is rapidly steering itself toward becoming a monopoly, at least on the internet.

As a result, *Google* has positioned itself as a vigorous rival with Amazon for buyer dollars with the debut of its Google Play, where publishers can offer their books for sale as ebooks.

But as I have discussed before, Google may not be the best place to sell books or ebooks either, since Google has also attracted numerous suits for its practice of scanning books in the public domain and also "orphan" rights books (books with no provenance of copyright) and offering them up free on the internet to read.

Google thinks that it can get away with piracy by dint of its money clout and its size, but at the same time it has attracted a reputation for being a pirate and most authors guarding their content rights are treating it as something to avoid. If you want to avoid any similar imperial entanglements I suggest you give both Google and Amazon wide berths.

The Attorney General of your state enforces the antitrust laws and acts upon any information indicating antitrust violations that affect the public. Such actions can include formal or informal investigation, and when necessary, a court action. In some cases, the Attorney General's Office may advise you that your issue should be directed to an appropriate district attorney or federal agency, or to private counsel for litigation in a lower tort court.

The Attorney General cannot act as a lawyer for, or give legal advice to, private individuals or businesses. Remember, the Attorney General stands ready to protect the citizens of the state and the economy on which they rely from illegal restraints of trade. However, this can only be done to the extent that concerned citizens help identify violations of law. To report a possible violation, contact the Attorney General's office in your state.

If you cannot engage your district attorney or copyright lawyer, I suggest you also contact the Federal Trade Commission (FTC) to report incidents you think qualify as antitrust violations.

ISBNs, LCCNs And Their Uses

The *ISBN*, or International Standard Book Number, is the most important thing you can have when it comes to presenting your book to booksellers for sale, especially when part of the steps to being published for sale involves having one. It is a code number designed for the unique and individual identification of your book, and distinguishes it from all other books or editions of the same title or author. It consists of a string of 13 numbers, grouped with hyphens, which compose a unique pattern. They also come in groups of 10 numbers, and some retailers may use those to identify books on their catalogs. The last number of these may be different on several bookselling sites owing to a check digit for inventory control. In this way, the uniqueness of the book is preserved and the information about it remains consistent as long as the book is available.

The number itself is *not* a legal requirement. It is only for the convenience of the booksellers you may wish to work with. Some booksellers will not buy your book for sale in their stores without a price having been fixed and printed both on the barcode and the back cover. Others don't care.

With online booksellers this does not appear to affect the listing or sale of your book in any way unless they require a number to conduct business. Even Amazon has recently relaxed its requirement of an ISBN in favor of its own ASIN, usually the ISBN-10, which is more readily distinguishable and easier to track for its Kindle ebooks, and only recognizes ISBNs on the printed books through one of its publishing sites; or if the author or publisher has already obtained one and it is readily printed on the book itself.

Books received through distribution platforms are required to have ISBNs at all times.

One can obtain an ISBN from *myidentifiers.com* (Bowker), the central agency responsible for issuing and registering the numbers, either singly or in a block of 10, 25, 100, or 1,000. After filling out an application one pays a fee by credit card or check and receives the number or block of numbers. This number or block of numbers is yours exclusively, and you may hold the number(s) indefinitely or use them over time at your discretion. There is no time limit to their use. If you think you will never publish more than 10 books, there is no obligation to buy more.

You can also order a *barcode*, an image file which contains the number and the price (optional). It is an optical code for the purpose of identifying the sale at bookstores just like you see on everything you buy. For a book, the barcode typically includes the ISBN at the top and displays it at the botton in a specific pattern. This is optional. Most book publishing services will insert the barcode for you at no charge after you have registered it.

Without a price, the barcode has a side code of *90000*, which is a replacement number. If you want to avoid having to republish every time you change the retail price, do not put a price on the cover. However, some booksellers will not take your book without it.

The barcode image usually goes on the lower right hand corner or center of the back cover within the ¼ inch safety margin.

A generic barcode image.

When applying text to your back cover, allow for a space of 2″ wide x 1.5″ high where the barcode image is to be inserted, near the right hand safety margin and just above the bottom safety margin; or just above the center and bottom. You also must list the ISBN somewhere on the cover of the book. I usually put it just below my contact information and my web site URL (user reference link).

You list the number and the book's details (metadata) on the *myidentifiers.com* site, which holds all the numbers you have bought. You are responsible for doing this. They are not a distributor but a bibliographic site booksellers and libraries consult for information about your book for **Books in Print**.

If not, and you have bought a distribution package through your favorite printer, the printer will begin this process for you. But I strongly recommend that you register and manage your own numbers because your printer can also enter details incorrectly or leave critical details off the listing. I know because it has happened to me just recently, and I had to go in and correct every single listing myself. Also, you can go in and change the metadata if you change your book's cover, its dimensions or other information.

Just in the last few months, Bowker has also branched into distribution services. I have not taken advantage because I already have a distributor. But it is a good thing to know when starting out.

Remember the only thing the ISBN gives you is *access*. It does not guarantee that your book will sell. That part is entirely up to you.

The **LCCN** (Library of Congress Certification Number) is a number assigned to a book by the U.S. Library of Congress and is not an ISBN, but if you want to have the book recorded as part of your copyright protection, you pay a small fee and send at least two copies of your book to them. They will assign the number after a review period. This number is far more permanent than an ISBN, as many books do not survive long enough and may be replaced by subsequent editions. It ensures that the book in its current form is properly registered. This is especially true of first edition hardcover books, but if your book is a paperback edition do not bother.

The **Universal Product Code** (UPC) is a barcode identifier, i.e.: a specific type of barcode that is widely used in North America and in countries including the UK, Australia, and New Zealand, for tracking trade items in stores. You can find out more about UPC from *www.barcodeinc.com*. They have put a free barcode generator on their site. While it is a little complicated to understand you can create a barcode for any product you care to sell, including books and ebooks, in place of the ISBN. The UPC is best for things you tend to produce in mass quantities and not relevant for one-offs.

A **QR code** is a new kind of identity stamp in use today and designed to be read on cell phones and tablet computers with cameras. It can be attached to anything you want to identify with its own unique marker, like a product code. It can be inserted into a picture, business card, label, shipping label, or anywhere you want a shopper to be able to pick up the code.

The code consists of black modules arranged in a square pattern on a white background. The information encoded can be text, URL or other data. An example is featured here:

Intellectual Property, Trademarks and Branding

As I discussed before, the issue of content ownership and control involves minding your backside every step of the way. So here I will discuss these important facets of publishing which you need to know before you do anything else.

Intellectual property is the product of your idea. It can be a specific product, image, video, film, video game, book, or whatever else you want to make and sell. The issues involved speak to whether your idea is original in scope; that is, not an exact copy or duplicate of anyone else's idea, and for which you have the right to own, usually expressed as a copyright. They can also relate to whichever idea or product you assign to someone else to create for you.

For example, Viacom, Inc. owns all the specific properties related to the television show *Star Trek*. They have assigned a copyright to every character, prop, design, music, logo (title), costume design and any other feature of the show. They have also assigned a copyright to every script for the show regardless of whether the script was produced. This means that fans of the show cannot copy or sell anything related to the show's images or characters for personal gain, and in the fan world the violation of copyrights are often frowned upon. Viacom can and will go after anyone who copies any facet of the show as it is. This is usually done by means of a *cease and desist* letter from their lawyers, and that is about all it takes.

In an unprecedented move, the producers of a film called **Galaxy Quest** (1999) were smart enough to change everything around. As a result, only fans familiar with the premise of *Star Trek* could recognize the telltale signs that this movie was a parody about the original series. The adventures of the actors in the fictional series was a masterpiece of portrayal including many of the running gags associated with the original show, and generated a fan following of its own. That it was good enough to be treated as a separate property has helped it to survive.

Another example: *Gucci* and *Louis Vuitton* bags and sunglasses are copied (bootlegged) with frequent regularity by fashion pirates who can make a lot of money selling cheap knockoffs (exact reproductions) of the original designs. In this case, the damages are quite extensive to the image of the designer's brand and caché in the fashion world, especially when the imitations are made so badly they fall apart, and their prices undercut the value of labor and effort expended on the design process.

But the pirates do not care about that. Once the bag is bought they move on, and the pirate shops are hastily erected stalls which can appear one day, disappear and then reappear later. Police intervention has been fruitless, since the pirates are sometimes supported by their customers, who would prefer to buy the knockoffs because they can.

Proprietary rights: This is treated a little differently. The owner of the property involved has received it as part of a contract for the labor involved in its design and creation. This means that no matter how much you are involved in the design process or its production, the piece *still does not belong to you*. You are an independent contractor to create the piece, but the design and everything related to it belongs to the company.

This particular assignment is common for products made by a large concern with a series of subsidiary products either related to each other or as part of a whole piece. It covers such things as computers, chips, circuits, programs, software, video games, location devices, disc players, automobiles, toys, and a whole panoply of other types of products.

Proprietary rights are attached to specific designs by means of patents, which detail the design specifics, appearance, components, blueprints, models and whatever else makes the piece specifically unique to that particular company.

For example, Apple launched a series of portable entertainment and communication devices, including an ereader. Everything which went into their design and creation is deemed proprietary, and Apple must own the patents associated with them. The hardware and software designers involved with their creation agreed to be paid for the labor and nothing else. Once the contract is completed, the end product belongs to Apple.

Occasionally you will hear of one company taking another to court for *patent infringement*. Many companies guard the chief sources and component designs of the products jealously. Industrial espionage is an ongoing battle for them, and as you have probably heard, some legal wars between companies are world famous. For example, the feuds between Coke® and Pepsi®, Apple® and Microsoft® (and now Google), and Popeyes® and Kentucky Fried Chicken®. Patents must be protected from theft at all times from imitators and those who develop a product design both independently and by coincidence.

The issue of *coincident design* happens very seldom. Usually the race to copyright designs occurs when one company seizes on an idea by reading about another's, and comes up with a design of their own to trump the application. It's all about both bragging rights and also claiming an important part of the consumer's pie.

The film *The Social Network* in 2010 presented a "biographical" story of Mark Zuckerberg's development of Facebook. While engaging in terms of presenting Zuckerberg as an overfocused cybergeek determined to create his own empire, I found it somewhat sketchy in terms of the actual details of the Winklevoss brothers' lawsuit and the truth about what drove Zuckerberg, portrayed as a bit of a hermit, to alienate his partners and friends without being aware of it.

He looked oblivious and superfocused, not awkward or shy. Toward the end of the film he does realize almost too late that his friends are what helped him to succeed. But Zuckerberg cannot be compared to Amazon's Jeff Bezos, whose personal story changes according to whim every single day.

Perhaps the most famous case of patent infringment occurred when Thomas Edison appropriated Nikola Tesla's plans for several devices, among which were the light bulb, alternating current, the wireless radio, and other devices, while Tesla worked for his company. Tesla submitted applications for the patents, including one for a death ray. Tesla was extremely secretive about his inventions, but Edison did not care about the results of his pilfering.

Tesla became mentally ill: paranoid, isolated, and anorexic, and when he died in 1943, (some say he was murdered for the death ray plans by the Russians) documents kept in a safe in his hotel room were removed and sent to his native home in Serbia. Several pages from a notebook critical to developing the death ray were torn out and are missing to this day.

Edison went on to found The Edison General Electric Company; which is called General Electric now, using Tesla's designs to create many of the appliances and controllers in use today.

This battle has recently been brought to the big screen with *The Current War* (2019), so I hardly need to expand on it here.

Trademarks - logos, images, or even words attached to the name of specific companies. Trademarks identify who the companies are and distinguish them as unique. They also take effect very much like copyrights, but most companies usually register them to make sure that there is no question of their legitimacy.

Violation of trademark rarely happens, but if the company has a stake in the stock market and is responsible for shareholders, it is in their interest to protect the symbol of their existence to protect against all other claims of ownership.

We are familiar with trademarks because they are all around us. The symbols for Exxon®, or Shell Oil®, or Alcoa Aluminum®, or Staples®, or Home Depot®, or Walmart®. These were designs which were thought out carefully and represent the companies and/or their products; even their long-term goals or overall specialty.

If by chance you want to become a small publisher or something bigger, it is in your interest to get yourself a trademark at some point in your business plan.

In 2013 I was forced to register my trademark logo for Antellus when I discovered that a Chinese investment company and cybersquatter wanted to buy not only all suffixes of my site's domain name, but also wanted to appropriate my logo for themselves. After a furious round of emails denying permission I sought a registration form and registered the mark. I have not heard from them since.

Here is some more information about trademarks, and I highly recommend you look into registering your logo when you are certain you are going to use it for a long time.

A trademark may be located on a package, a label, a voucher or on the product itself. For the sake of corporate identity, trademarks are also displayed on company owned buildings. The unauthorized usage of trademarks by producing and trading counterfeit consumer goods is known as brand piracy.

The owner of a trademark may pursue legal action against trademark infringement. Most countries require formal registration of a trademark as a precondition for pursuing this type of action. The United States, Canada and other countries also recognize common law trademark rights, which means action can be taken to protect an unregistered trademark if it is in use. Still, common law trademarks offer the holder in general less legal protection than registered trademarks.

A trademark may be designated by the following symbols:

^{TM} : an unregistered trademark, which is used to promote or brand goods;

SM : an unregistered service mark, which is used to promote or brand services;

® : a registered trademark.

There is also a range of nonconventional trademarks comprising marks which do not fall into these standard categories, such as those based on a color, smell, or sound (like jingles or signature music).

The term "trademark" is also used informally to refer to any distinguishing attribute by which an individual is identified, such as the characteristics of celebrities and celebrity names. The late musician Prince once employed a trademark design to identify himself, but later dropped it because "it was too hard to pronounce".

When a trademark is used in relation to services rather than products, it may sometimes be called a service mark, particularly in the United States.

Fundamental concepts: The essential function of a trademark is to *exclusively* identify the commercial source or origin of products or services, so a trademark as properly called, indicates source or serves as a badge of origin. Certain exclusive rights attach to a registered mark, which can be enforced by an action for trademark infringement, while unregistered trademark rights may be enforced pursuant to the common law in tort cases. It should be noted that trademark rights generally arise out of the use of, or to maintain exclusive rights over, that particular sign in relation to certain products or services, assuming there are no other trademark objections.

History: Bass Brewery's logo became the first image to be registered as a trademark, in 1875. It is said that blacksmiths who made swords in the Roman Empire are thought of as being the first users of trademarks. Other notable trademarks that have been used for a long time include Löwenbräu, which claims use of its lion mark since 1383.

The first trademark legislation was passed by the Parliament of England under the reign of King Henry III in 1266, which required all bakers to use a distinctive mark for the bread they sold.

The first modern trademark laws emerged in the late 19th century. In France the first comprehensive trademark system in the world was passed into law in 1857 with the "Manufacture and Goods Mark Act". In Britain, the 1862 Merchandise Marks Act made it a criminal offense to imitate another's trade mark with the intent to defraud or to enable another to defraud. In 1875 the Trade Marks Registration Act was passed which allowed formal registration of trade marks at the UK Patent Office for the first time.

The 1875 Act defined a registrable trademark as a device, or mark, or name of an individual or firm printed in some particular and distinctive manner; or a written signature or copy of a written signature of an individual or firm; or a distinctive label or ticket.

Registration was considered to comprise prima facie evidence of ownership of a trademark, and registration of marks began in 1876. In the United States, Congress first attempted to establish a federal trademark regime in 1870. This statute purported to be an exercise of Congress' Copyright Clause powers. However, the Supreme Court struck down the 1870 statute later on in the decade.

In 1881, Congress passed a new trademark act, this time pursuant to its Commerce Clause powers. Congress revised the Trademark Act in 1905.

The Trademarks Act of 1938 in the United Kingdom set up the first registration system based on the "intent-to-use" principle. The Act also established an application publishing procedure and expanded the rights of the trademark holder to include the barring of trademark use even in cases where confusion remained unlikely. This Act served as a model for similar legislation elsewhere.

In the United States, a design mark with an eagle and a ribbon and the words "Economical, Brilliant" was the first registered trademark, filed by the Averill Chemical Paint Company on August 30, 1870 under the Trademark Act of 1870. However, the U.S. Supreme Court held the 1870 Act to be unconstitutional.

The oldest U.S. registered trademark still in use is a depiction of the Biblical figure Samson wrestling a lion, registered in the United States on May 27, 1884 by the J.P. Tolman Company (now Samson Rope Technologies, Inc.).

In 1923, the businessman and author Edgar Rice Burroughs registered his fictitious character Tarzan as a trademark even after the copyright to the Tarzan story expired. His company used ownership of the trademarks relating to the character which, unlike copyrights, do not have a limited length, to control the production of media using its imagery and to license the character for use in other works such as adaptations. This practice is a precursor to the modern concept of a media franchise.

In 1980, there were fewer than 10,000 registered high tech trademarks in the United States. In 2011, there were more than 300,000.

Symbols: The two symbols associated with U.S. trademarks ™ (trademark) and ® (registered trademark) represent the status of a mark and accordingly its level of protection. While ™ can be used with any common law usage of a mark, ® may only be used by the owner of a mark following registration with the relevant national authority, such as the U.S. Patent and Trademark Office (USPTO or PTO). The proper manner to display either symbol is immediately following the mark in superscript style.

Terminology: Terms such as "mark", "brand" and "logo" are sometimes used interchangeably with "trademark". It must be a graphical representation and must be applied to all goods or services for which it is registered. Specialized types of trademark include certification marks, collective trademarks and defensive trademarks.

A trademark which is popularly used to describe a product or service, rather than to distinguish the product or services from those of third parties, is sometimes known as a genericized trademark. If such a mark becomes synonymous with that product or service, to the extent that the trademark owner can no longer enforce its proprietary rights, the mark becomes generic.

A "trademark look" is an informal term for a characteristic look for a performer or character of some sort. It is usually not legally trademark protected and the term is not used in the trademark law.

Registration: The law considers a trademark to be a form of property. Proprietary rights in relation to a trademark may be established through actual use in the marketplace, or through registration of the mark with the trademarks office or "trademarks registry" of a particular jurisdiction. In some jurisdictions, trademark rights can be established through either or both means.

Certain jurisdictions generally do not recognize trademarks rights arising through their use. If the trademark owners do not hold registrations for their marks in those jurisdictions, the extent to which they will be able to enforce their rights will be limited.

In the United States, the registration process includes several steps. First, the trademark owner files an application to register the trademark. About three months after it is filed, the application is reviewed by an examining attorney at the U.S. Patent and Trademark Office (USPTO). The examining attorney checks for compliance with the rules of the Trademark Manual of Examination Procedure.

This review includes procedural matters such as making sure the applicant's goods or services are identified properly. It also includes more substantive matters such as making sure the applicant's mark is not merely descriptive or likely to cause confusion with a pre-existing mark. If the application runs afoul of any requirement, the examining attorney will issue an office action requiring the applicant to address certain issues or refusals prior to registration of the mark. If the examining attorney approves the application, it will be "published for opposition" for a period of 30 days.

During this 30 day period, other parties who may be affected by the registration of the trademark may step forward to file an Opposition Proceeding to stop the registration of the mark. If an Opposition proceeding is filed, it brings a case before the Trademark Trial and Appeal Board to determine both the validity of the grounds for the opposition as well as the ability of the applicant to register the mark at issue.

Finally, provided that no other party opposes the registration of the mark during the opposition period or the opposition is ultimately decided in the applicant's favor, the mark will be registered.

Outside of the United States, the registration process is substantially similar to that found in the U.S. save for one notable exception in many countries: registration occurs once an application is reviewed by an examiner and found to be entitled to registration. A registration certificate is issued subject to the mark being open to opposition for a period of typically 6 months from the date of registration.

The law in most jurisdictions also allows the owner of a registered trademark to prevent unauthorized use of the mark in relation to products or services which are identical or similar to the "registered" products or services; and in certain cases, prevent its use in relation to entirely dissimilar products or services. The test is always whether a consumer of the goods or services will be confused as to the identity of the source or origin.

An example may be a very large multinational brand such as "Sony" where a product such as a pair of sunglasses might be assumed to have come from Sony Corporation of Japan, even if it is not part of a class of goods that Sony has any rights to.

Once trademark rights are established in a particular jurisdiction, these rights are generally only enforceable in that jurisdiction, a quality which is sometimes known as territoriality. However, there is a range of international trademark laws and systems which facilitate the protection of trademarks in more than one jurisdiction.

Search parameters: In the United States, the USPTO maintains a database of registered trademarks. The database is open to the public. A licensed attorney may be required to interpret the search results. As trademarks are governed by federal law, state law, and common law, a thorough search as to the availability of a mark is very important.

In the United States, obtaining a trademark search and relying upon the results of an opinion issued by an attorney may insulate a trademark user from being required to pay treble damages and attorney's fees in a trademark infringement case; as it demonstrates that the trademark user performed due diligence and was using the mark in good faith.

The USPTO internally captures more information about trademarks than what they publicly disclose on their official search website, such as the complete contents of every logo trademark filing. Trademarks may also be searched on third-party databases.

In Europe, and if a community trademark has to be filed, searches have to be conducted with the OHIM or Community Trademark Office and with the various national offices. An alternative solution is to conduct a trademark search within private databases.

Classification systems exist to help in searching for marks. One example is the "International Classification of the Figurative Elements of Marks", better known as the Vienna Classification.

Ability to register: Trademark rights must be maintained through the actual lawful use of the trademark. These rights will cease if a mark is not actively used for a period of time, normally 5 years. In the case of a trademark registration, failure to actively use the mark in the lawful course of trade, or to enforce the registration in the event of infringement, may also expose the registration itself to become liable for an application for the removal from the register after a certain period of time if the mark has not been used.

An owner can at any time commence action for infringement against a third party as long as the owner follows through to take action within a reasonable period of time, called "acquiescence". The owner can always reserve the right to take legal action until a court decides that the third party had gained notoriety which the owner *must* have been aware of. It will be for the third party to prove that their use of the mark is substantial as it is the onus of a company using a mark to check they are not infringing previously registered rights.

In the U.S., failure to use a trademark for the period of time paid for, aside from the corresponding impact on product quality, will result in abandonment of the mark, whereby any party may use the mark. An abandoned mark is not irrevocably in the public domain, but may be registered by any party which has established exclusive and active use of it, and must be associated or linked with the original mark owner.

Unlike other forms of intellectual property, a registered trademark can last forever, theorietically. So long as a trademark's use is continuous, a trademark holder may keep the mark registered with the U.S. Patent and Trademark Office by filing a Section 8 Affidavit of Continuous Use as well as Section 9 applications for renewal, as required about every 5 and 10 years.

Enforcing rights: The extent to which a trademark owner may prevent unauthorized use of trademarks depends on various factors.

Unauthorized use of a registered trademark need not be intentional in order for infringement to occur, though damages in an infringement lawsuit will generally be greater if there was any intention to deceive.

A growing area of law relating to the enforcement of trademark rights is called "secondary liability", which allows for assigning of liability to one who has not acted directly to infringe a trademark, but whose legal responsibility may arise under the doctrines of liability.

Limits and defenses to claims of infringement: Trademark is subject to various defenses, such as abandonment, limitations on geographic scope, and fair use. In the United States, the fair use defense protects many of the interests in free expression related to those protected by the First Amendment. Fair use may be asserted on two grounds: either that the alleged infringer is using the mark to describe accurately an aspect of its products, or that the alleged infringer is using the mark to identify the mark owner.

An example: although Maytag owns the trademark "Whisper Quiet", makers of other products may describe their goods as being "whisper quiet" so long as these products do not fall under the same category of goods the trademark is protected under.

Another example: Audi can run advertisements saying that a trade publication has rated an Audi model higher than a BMW model, since they are only using "BMW" to identify the competitor.

In a related sense, an auto mechanic can advertise that he services Volkswagens, and a former Playboy Playmate of The Year can identify herself as such on her website.

Wrongful or groundless threats of infringement: Various jurisdictions have laws which are designed to prevent trademark owners from making wrongful threats of trademark infringement action against other parties. These laws are intended to prevent large or powerful companies from intimidating or harassing smaller companies. Where one party makes a threat to sue another for trademark infringement, the threat may itself become a basis for legal action. In this situation, the party receiving such a threat may seek a declaratory judgment from the Court.

Trademark law is designed to fulfill the public policy objective of consumer protection by preventing the public from being misled as to the origin or quality of a product or service. By identifying the commercial source of products and services, trademarks facilitate identification of products and services which meet the expectations of consumers as to quality and other characteristics.

Trademarks may also serve as an incentive for manufacturers, providers or suppliers, to consistently provide quality products or services in order to maintain their business reputation.

Furthermore, if a trademark owner does not maintain quality control and adequate supervision in relation to the manufacture and provision of products or services supplied by a licensee, such "naked licensing" will eventually adversely affect the owner's rights.

By the same token, trademark holders must be cautious in the sale of their mark for similar reasons when applying to license. When assigning an interest in a trademark, if the associated product or service is not transferred with it, then this may be an "assignment-in-gross" and could lead to a loss of rights in the trademark.

Companies will often contract with the sellers to help transition the mark and goods or services to the new owners to ensure the continuity of the trademark.

Trademarks, patents and designs collectively form a subset of intellectual property known as "industrial property" because they are often created and used in an industrial or commercial context.

Copyright Laws: By comparison, copyright law generally seeks to protect original literary, artistic and other creative works. Continued active use and periodic renewal of registration can make a trademark perpetual, whereas copyright usually lasts for the duration of the author's lifespan plus 70 years for works by individuals; and some limited time after creation for works by corporate entities. This can lead to confusion in cases where a work passes into the public domain but the character in question remains a registered trademark.

Although intellectual property laws such as these are theoretically distinct, more than one type may afford protection to the same article.

For example, the particular design of a bottle may qualify for copyright protection as a nonutilitarian item, or for trademark protection based on its shape, or the appearance of the bottle as a whole may be protectable.

Titles and character names from books or movies may also be protectable as trademarks while the works from which they are drawn may qualify for copyright protection as a whole. Trademark protection does not apply to the utilitarian features of a product such as the plastic interlocking studs on Lego bricks.

Drawing these distinctions is necessary, but often challenging, especially in jurisdictions where patents and copyrights pass into the public domain.

By comparison with a trademark, patents and copyrights cannot be abandoned and a patent holder or copyright owner can generally enforce its rights without taking any particular action to maintain the patent or copyright. Additionally, patent holders and copyright owners may not necessarily need to actively police their rights.

However, a failure to bring a timely infringement suit or action against a known infringer may give the defendant a defense of implied consent when such a suit is finally brought. Like patents and copyrights, trademarks can be bought, sold, and transferred from one company or another. Unlike patents and copyrights, trademarks may not remain intact through this process.

Where trademarks have been acquired for the purpose of marketing generic products, courts have refused to enforce them.

A trademark becomes diluted when the use of similar or identical trademarks in other markets means that the trademark will lose its capacity to signify a single source. In other words, unlike ordinary trademark law, dilution protection extends to trademark uses that do not confuse consumers regarding who has made a product.

Instead, dilution protection law aims to protect sufficiently strong trademarks from losing their association in the public mind with a particular product, perhaps imagined if the trademark were to be encountered independently of any product: e.g., just the word "Pepsi" spoken or on a billboard. Under trademark law, dilution occurs either when unauthorized use of a mark "blurs" the distinctive nature of the mark or tarnishes it.

In the United States, trademark registration can only be sold and assigned if accompanied by the sale of an underlying asset.

Licensing: Getting a permit from the trademark owner to license the use of the trademark to a third party in order to enable the commercial use of the trademark legally, which is a contract form between the two parties and has all the policy and content scope as defined. The licensor must monitor the quality of the goods being produced by the licensee to avoid the risk of trademark being deemed abandoned by the courts.

A trademark license should therefore include appropriate provisions dealing with quality control, whereby the licensee provides warranties as to quality and the licensor has rights to inspection and monitoring.

Domain names: The advent of the domain name system has led to attempts by trademark holders to enforce their rights over domain names that are similar or identical to their existing trademarks, particularly by seeking control over the domain names at issue.

As with dilution protection, enforcing trademark rights over domain name owners involves protecting a trademark outside the obvious context of its consumer market, because domain names are global and not limited by goods or service. This conflict is easily resolved when the domain name owner actually uses the domain to compete with the trademark owner.

Cybersquatting, however, does not involve competition. Instead, an unlicensed user registers a domain name identical to a trademark, and offers to sell the domain to the trademark owner. Typosquatters, those registering common misspellings of trademarks as domain names, have also been targeted successfully in trademark infringement suits. "Gripe sites", on the other hand, tend to be protected as free speech, and are therefore more difficult to attach claims as trademark infringement.

This clash of the new technology with existing trademark rights resulted in several high profile decisions as the courts of many countries tried to coherently address the issue within the framework of existing trademark law.

Initial interest confusion refers to customer confusion that creates an interest in a competitor's "product"; or in the online context, another party's website. Even though initial interest confusion is dispelled by the time any actual sales occur, it allows a trademark infringer to capitalize on the good will associated with the original mark.

In addition, courts have upheld the rights of trademark owners with regard to commercial use of domain names, even in cases where goods sold there legitimately bear the mark.

In the landmark decision *Creative Gifts, Inc. v. UFO*, 235 F.3d 540, defendants had registered the domain name "Levitron.com" to sell goods bearing the trademark "Levitron" under an at will license from the trademark owner. The 10th Circuit Court of New Mexico affirmed the rights of the trademark owner with regard to the domain name, despite all promises to stop by the offenders.

Most courts particularly frown on cybersquatting, and find that this practice was itself a sufficiently commercial use, i.e., "trafficking" in trademarks, to reach into the area of trademark infringement. Most jurisdictions have since amended their trademark laws to address domain names specifically, and to provide explicit remedies against cybersquatters.

In the United States, the legal situation was clarified by the **Anticybersquatting Consumer Protection Act** (ACPA), 15 U.S.C. § 1125(d), a U.S. law enacted in 1999 that established a cause of action for registering, trafficking in, or using a domain name confusingly similar to, or dilutive of, a trademark or personal name. It is an amendment to the Lanham Act, which explicitly prohibits cybersquatting; defining it as "occurring when a person other than the trademark holder registers the domain name of a well known trademark and then attempts to profit from this by either ransoming the domain name back to the trademark holder, or using the domain name to divert business from the trademark holder to the domain name holder."

This international legal change has also led to the creation of ICANN Uniform Domain-Name Dispute Resolution Policy (UDRP) and other dispute policies for specific countries which attempt to streamline the process of resolving who should own a domain name without dealing with other infringement issues such as damages.

This is particularly desirable to trademark owners when the domain name registrant may be in another country or even anonymous to the original domain owner.

As with other trademarks, the domain name will not be subject to registration unless the proposed mark is actually used to identify the registrant's goods or services to the public, rather than simply being the location on the Internet where the applicant's web site appears. *Amazon.com* is a prime example of a protected trademark for a domain name central to the public's identification of the company and its products.

Among trademark practitioners there remains a great deal of debate around trademark protection. World Trademark Review has been reporting on the fiery discussion between trademark owners and domain suppliers, who are only out to make money from anyone wanting to buy the domain space.

Like any national law, trademark laws apply only in their applicable country or jurisdiction, a quality which is sometimes known as "territoriality". The inherent limitations of the territorial application of trademark laws have been mitigated by various intellectual property treaties.

I could go on for more pages about this, but I hope you will carefully research the aspects of using a trademark to protect your own business and competitive advantage online and off.

Brand or Logo. See *Trademark*. The difference is that you must produce a public image which will last and ensure customer confidence. Many authors confuse branding with the trademark. But as an author, your name alone *can be* your brand if you choose to use it that way. As a self-publisher I brand my books with my publishing trademark; that is, I let my imprint represent me, even if every book I write has my name on it. In that case, my brand logo *is* my trademark, and I maintain my book site with that logo displayed on the very top of the front page.

So you see, there are many things you can do with your book once it is published. The rest is up to you. But don't be discouraged if you encounter problems like I have outlined. Go forward with your head held high, and your confidence will rub off on others.

The Future of Publishing

As the century unfolds, we have seen an unprecedented explosion in ways to publish a book, ebook or other kinds of media. In 2001 we were plunged into war, mourning a multitude of victims of terrorism, losing our marketing power to a series of drop offs of intellectual capacity and production expertise as companies outsourced people by the thousands. But in all of that, the voracius appetite of book readers never fell short. The need for stories, textbooks and guides has never been stronger than now.

Since 2003, as I have said before there had been an acceleration of developments to make books available everywhere. The ease and convenience of taking your whole library with you on a train, bus or airplane has created a new and growing demand for ebooks and the devices made to read them on.

To meet this demand, publishers must recognize the value of printing books on demand as a solution to their costs to print, rendering them more able to sell a book than with conventional methods, which are frought with obstacles. They can then set their retail prices more in line with consumer demand. True, this does not work for all books, but for novels and nonfiction books with little or no special properties, there is a true opportunity for anyone with a story to tell to publish and sell it in the form of an ebook.

No longer do a mere handful of publishers control the type of books we can buy and read. As more and more people bypass them to self-publish, or create markets which host independent booksellers of niche markets, the larger companies are slowly learning that it is no longer business as usual. Unless they begin to compete with the smaller booksellers, they will be left behind. Some are only now acting to catch up.

It is true that some books were designed to be produced and sold the old fashioned way. They will continue to attract the enjoyment of people who like books for their collectible and intrinsic artistic values. The introduction of print on demand and ebook formats will only make literature more accessible to those who cannot afford to pay for an expensive textbook or hardback novel.

As more software is developed to make reading user friendly, a great many more people will realize their dream of being published. We should not fear the coming decade, as it will expand literacy and education to the whole world. Knowledge is power, and those who know how to use it have the advantage. The powerful got that way by reading as much as they could. The balance to the abuse of power is the number of people with the same knowledge, because ignorance makes slaves of us all.

MARKETING, ADVERTISING AND PROMOTION

How to Identify Your Market

Now that you have a brand spanking new book to sell, the most important part of your marketing work involves finding the right category to list it in. The bookselling world is highly dependent on a rigorous heirarchy of categories or *genres*. Many book stores place books on their shelves according to their popularity or their subjects; and some are paid to place them in specific sections of their store by publishers with big advertising budgets.

If you look on any of the shopping sites you will see that *Books* occupy one of many other categories, and as a category it is immediately subdivided into two categories: *Fiction* and *Nonfiction*. Sometimes they are lumped together into the most popular, among which are Literature, Art, History, Philosophy, Science, Self-Help, Life and Style, Fantasy, Horror, Mystery, Romance and Science Fiction.

To aid in categorizing books according to subject, a series of numbers have been developed and maintained by the BISAC group. BISAC is an acronym for **Book Industry Standards and Communications**. The official definition of the term is an industry-approved "list of standard subjects designed for use in the book trade in the U.S. and English-Speaking Canada."

Meaning, these codes are used to properly "shelve" your title at retailers.

Whatever your book is about it must fit neatly into one of these. If you are not sure where it will go, or it crosses two or all of them, you can stick the title into Literature and be done with it. But Literature is a broad category which includes the classics and also books which do not fall neatly into any other category. Your book can easily get lost in the alphabet soup of titles. It is alright to mention it as a subcategory. There is a new and often ignored category called *Speculative Fiction* which many booksellers do not acknowledge yet, but there is also a number for that.

If you want to reach more readers who will really like your book, you have to get a bit more specific. When your target market is narrowed down it will be easier for readers to find your title within the range of their interests. Once you have a clear idea who to market to, the next step to reaching them is clear.

Use a Web Site to Achieve Maximum Potential

The next and most important part of your marketing work aside from the usual advertising channels involves setting up your presence on the *world wide web*. The internet is by far the most viable and least expensive connection you will have between you and your reading market. More and more shoppers are turning to the internet for their needs, so it is vitally important that you acqaint yourself with it and how it works.

You must become competitive with the booksellers in order to drive sales, and they are in competition with you already. Many have their own shopping sites set up. They will undercut you on the list price for your own book (like *Amazon*), so you have to work harder to make sure the shoppers see you first. You can even discount the list price of your book to make it more attractive to buyers, but never discount below the cost to print and wholesale commissions, or you will never make any money yourself.

There are several ways you can link in and gain recognition for your work without waiting for all those retailing sites to sell the book for you.

The least expensive way is to join a **social network** or **book marketing** site where you can have your own page for free. They include Facebook, Twitter, BookWorks, Book Blogs, The Book Marketing Network, Booklife (a promotion arm of Publishers' Weekly), and others. Once you sign up, you can create a profile which identifies you, your goals or a brief biography, add a blog about your books and where to get them. But there are no automatic buy buttons or selling features to the page. It is simply a way to get the word out. If you are keen about selling you can upload a cover image and describe it with a link to the buy button on whichever shopping site you prefer.

The second and more useful is to list your book on a **book listing site** or on what is called a "paying marketplace" where you have the option to sell your books directly on their site through their buy buttons. They are set up to do the bookkeeping involved. If you are content with that, you need do nothing more. But be prepared to wait a long time before a single copy is sold.

Lulu offers a storefront but you have to let people know it is there, and you cannot enter into wholesale agreements with sellers and be able to price your book competitively. But they are the least expensive option overall.

The third and **best** way to get your book noticed is to *buy a domain name* and run your own website. Here is where you can establish yourself as a legitimate writer and be able to create a brand around your name or your publishing logo, how your site will look, and so on. The best way to be recognized as a publisher is to establish a brand name and name the domain with that.

You can modify your site by adding as many pages to it as you need to. The domain name should cost no more than about $15 per year to register. The site's DNS (Domain Name Server) web hosting service costs about the same or more per year and includes email hosting and other features. The minimum amount of space is about 5GB (gigabytes). If you need more space you can get it for a small add-on fee.

For example: my web site, *www.antellus.com*, includes each book I sell and their attendant buy buttons. The links are the actual pages about the books, preview samples, and so on. I have done the same with my jewelry and art. I have access to 5 mailboxes for an additional fee but I go with just the one, and a lot of storage space to start with so I have a long way to go before I have to spend any more money. The hosting server and domain registrar includes a certification registry and yearly billing for my web hosting space.

Recently, in order to get your web site listed on search engines like Google and Bing, you must purchase an additional SSL certificate, which will render your site secure for listing. The site URL must include the header *https://* instead of http://, so any add-on feature of your web hosting should include that.

In many cases the search engine your email address is attached to: Yahoo, Google, or Bing, hosts a minisite you can use to promote your work. Depending on your particular need there is a whole raft of possibilities, and for a low cost you can start a small home-based business of your own.

If you know more about HTML already you can skip past this section.

The Basics of HTML

HTML is the most basic coding language on the web and the most often used. Some sites use *LINUX,* or *bbcode,* or are encoded entirely in *Javascript* and *C++;* but HTML is the easiest to learn. Those pages did not create themselves or appear like magic. Someone sat down and had to craft the page by typing in the code and placing a series of tags in a specific order.

If you are not that computer savvy it is still possible for you to begin a page by copying the code from another site and then filling in all the information you want your page to say. I taught myself HTML through a series of manuals and practice, and now 10 years later I can code without looking up any of the information. I keep up with the latest devlopments in coding so that my work is seamless with more sophisticated devices.

It seems like hard work, but once you learn how a page gets put together the basics will be easy. You craft HTML in a text editor, and using the basic codes you can copy and paste as many pieces of a given code module at once. Some parts of the code are not necessary at all and you can get by without them.

To start an HTML page you must open a TXT file first. You can use Notepad or Wordpad for this. For basic HTML pages you can start by using all caps inside a tag (< >). For some advanced forms of HTML you are required to code entirely in lower case but I will start you off with the basics.

The first tag to place on the page is <HTML>. This is the most simple and rudimentary form of the tag. The next tag is <HEAD>. This defines the header for the document. Inside this tag you then define the <TITLE>, the <META> description tags, the keywords, the base anchor URL for the site, and the style sheet, usually defined inside the <STYLE> tag. Other information like your name and address can be included, but to avoid identity theft I would avoid using the address at all. But <AUTHOR> is still a good way to identify yourself.

Here is a sample of the header as it appears in its simplest form. Most HTML forms are now composed in all lower case:

```
<!DOCTYPE html> (good for XHTML and HTML5)
<html>
<head>
<title>My Web Page</title>
```

<lang="EN"/> good if you are in the US or UK, Canada and other English sourced sites

<meta charset="UTF-8"/>

<meta name="viewport" content="width=device-width, initial-scale=1.0"/>

<meta name="robots" content="index, nofollow"/>

<base href="http://www.yoursite.com/your-products"/> or this and a subbase file name.

If you must create files for the HTML5 subset of web pages, you insert the viewport meta tag thus:

<meta name="viewport" content="userscalable=no, width=device-width"/>

<meta content="yes" name="apple-mobile-web-app-capable"/>.

<meta type="description" content="a web page dedicated to my book"/>

<meta type="keywords" content="keywords related to your book"/>

<meta type="author" content="your name or company name"/> This is optional.

<style>

body { color: #000000; font-family: Verdana, Helvetica, sans-serif; font-size: 20px; background: #xxxxxx; } Note that there is a forward and trailing blank space in the coding between { and }.

h1 { color: #bbbbbb; font-size: 24px; weight: (medium or bold) } (*the normal number of headlines is 6*)

You can also craft specific features of the site using a term and then coding its parameters. <price>, <border>, etc. can all be specified here. In phone apps, an additional parameter called "img" will specify how your images are seen on a phone. As follows:

img { max-width: 100%; height: auto }

link { color: #xxxxxx }

vlink { color: #xxxxxx }

</style>

</head>

The trailing forward slash in the *meta* tags is a feature which relates to versions of XHTML 1.0 or higher. In the latest transitional form of the code all the tags are in lower case and all attributes or conditions *must* be enclosed in quote marks.

The <link> tag is a new feature designed to assign a preference for a particular page in search engines. You can use this for pages you want to be selected first or in the case of multiple pages of the same content, but which were named something else earlier. SEO specialists say you should use the tag so the older pages will not come up first.

The colors designated in the <style> tag are based on hexadecimal codes for specific color groups and can be changed to anything else as long as you keep them to groups of 6 numeric characters or colors. The lowest number possible is *black* or #000000, while the highest number is *white* at #FFFFFF. The hashtag is necessary to define the color in hex.

However, be careful with this. *Link* refers to the color any link on your site will appear in. *Vlink* refers to the color the last visited link will appear in. I have defined my link and vlink parameters, but the browser in use determines how they are displayed.

If you visit a site which has a link, the link will change to that color when the page has been read and you return to the other page. Note that you do not need a trailing slash, because it will be closed with the </body> tag.

If you are not using any background color but white, you can even leave off the background color definition. The default color for the text is black, so you can even leave off the color definition for the font. But in order for it to pass the w3c.org HTML validator you should leave them on.

Next is the <body> tag, which defines the actual start and interior of your page. The area following this tag is where you actually insert your details. You can even define how the links on your site will appear. In order to center the information on your page, you insert a <center> tag to enclose all details, concluding with a </center> tag, before you close with </html>.

Here are some of the tags you need to use to define what your page will look like apart from what you put in the header. Many other site developers prefer to use the <div> tag but it turns out that many internet browsers may not be able to read the tags. A recent article by an expert said that all you need is a series of tables to divide pieces of displayed information. So now I only use tables and they read on my pages fine. Here is the code:

<table> sets up a table

<th> defines the first row of labels for the table, but in most cases it is not necessary.

<tr> defines a table row. You can define a background color for it and even define the row's height in number of pixels.

<td> defines a cell in the row. You can modify it with alignment parameters and define a background color for it. To center any information stored in the cell data, you can use the <center></center> tags.

<p> and </p> defines a paragraph. You can modify it with subtags which sets how the paragraph will appear.

</td> closes the cell.

</tr> closes the row.

</th> closes the header.

</table> closes the table.

Other tags include:

 Carriage return. This is a self closing tag so it needs to be set with a trailing slash.

<img src="URL/image.suffix" alt="xyz"/> defines an image to be inserted. Inside this tag you can modify most attributes of the image, including its width, height, alignment, and define a border for it. Unfortunately, nobody has seen fit to craft a modifier which allows one to define the border *color* in the image tag; just the size. The default border size in an image tag is "1". The *suffix* is the image's format: JPG, BMP, TIF, or PNG. Note that the trailing slash is required for all image tags without a corresponding closing tag.

When you have finished with your tags you must make sure they are closed according to the rules. Then you finish with closing tags for the whole document:

</body>

</html>

Save the TXT file as an .htm or .html file. This will lock the code into place and create the page. This saves as the base page. You can then keep the text file open while you work with the coding protocols to modify it. In order to lock in the code you must save your work each time, then refresh the web page to see how it looks. If you're not sure, you can copy the source code for a simple web site and see it in action.

Do not get confused about extra blank spaces in the text file; they do not actually affect the coding or appearance of the final product in any way. It is only the arrangement and sequence of the code lines which matter. Some web sites are coded with a series of indentations for each line which are actually superfluous for me. I prefer a straight list, but if you like the indentations you are perfectly free to use them.

Here is a sample of what I work with, since it is easy for me to build a page from scratch. I use the transitional XHMTL coding protocols, so to prevent confusion I will not start with the opening tag, but present the sequence in order after it. The spaces between lines are for illustrative use. They are not necessary to coding a proper page.

```
<head>
<title>My Web Page</title>
<meta charset="UTF-8"/>
<meta name="robots" content="noindex, nofollow"/>
<meta name="viewport" content="userscalable=no, width=device-
width"/>
<meta content="yes" name="apple-mobile-web-app-capable"/>
<base href="https://www.antellus.com/mobile/books"/>
<meta type="description" content="this is my web page, where I
place my books for sale"/>
<meta type="robots" content="index, all"/>
```
This is optional. You can also use a text file, robots.text, which describes how your site can be crawled by server robots.
```
<meta type="keywords" content="books, ebooks, marketing, selling,
retail, shopping"/>
<style>
    body { font-family: Verdana, Helvetica, sans-serif; font-size: 20px
}
    h1 { color: #bbbbbb; font-size: 20px; font-weight: bold }
```
Headlines are stated from 1 to 6 in the order they are presented. You can also define the line-height if necessary.
```
</style>
</head>
<body>
<table>
```
In later versions of HTML cellspacing and cellpadding attributes are not necessary if they are 0. That is usually the default setting.
```
<tr>
<td>
```

<center> Content beyond this point is then centered on the page.
<table> sets up an interior table
<tr>
<td>
<center>
<img src="my URL/images/xanadu.jpg" alt="xanadu" ("alt" is used to identify the image for site crawlers) border="1" /></td>

Alternately: <img src="xanadu.jpg" width="300" alt=""/> if you want your image to be seen on a cellphone. The "alt" is left blank because alt descriptions fill up more space. Similarly, a border is not necessary unless the image has more white along the edges. the img parameter in the <style> list will restrict the image size to 300 pixels wide for iPhones or Android phones.
</center></td>
<td><p>I put some text here if I want to.</p> (<p> can be left, centered, justified, or right) </td>
(If I want to add more rows or cells I can do so here. The inner table is inside the area defined by the opening table of the body and will not go past it.)
</tr></table> This closes the inner inner table.
</center></td></tr></table> This closes the outer table, and sets it apart from the rest of the page text.
<p>I can even put text or information outside the inner table</p>
</td></tr></table> Closes the page setting table.
</body>
</html>

And there you have a basic page coded in HTML. If you are bold enough to try using the transitional formats or want to really get involved with it, the tutorials on *w3c.org* will get you set up and going. I am only presenting what it looks like at its most basic level. It's up to you to learn how to code a web page yourself.

No matter where you start, here are some key elements to the web site and what it should look like so it will draw readers to you:

The *front page* – usually designated as the index page, *index.html*. Here you should have a side or top bar showing the logo and main links which connect the front page to the rest of the site. It serves as your sitemap page if you choose not to use one. Here is where you can determine the color of the background, your color theme and common typeface or font, the placement of your features and the look of professionalism you want to project.

This is where you also provide the site crawler on any search engine with the keywords and description for the site by use of the *meta tags*. Always include the title of your book in a tag along with your own name or author name, including any and all keywords associated with the book's subject and some of the related subjects it might cover.

But be careful with this. Recent discoveries indicate that if you use *too many* keywords in the meta tag the search engine's crawler will become confused and bypass your site altogether. The only way to get around that is to list as much information as you can in the body of the page and restrict your keywords only to those which are most relevant.

The most important features on the page should be the book's cover, description and reviews, if any; and the links to your buy buttons, or all the books you sell and links to their product pages. If you prefer you can include links to any retailer sites that sell your products but I have to warn you that the best way to sell them is to drive traffic to your site and don't worry about what the other sites are doing. They are certainly not worried about you.

I have seen other sites where the web master has filled the front page with clutter. Not just advertising clutter but personal clutter. Flash animation and popup ads, banners advertising other books or products, bright and jarring colors, **HUGE HEADLINES or Type**, photos of relatives, and oodles of space in between key portions, forcing people to scroll down farther to see the rest. The in-your-face approach to site design is not good for selling any product, and some have actually written the book around a completely different product altogether. Viewers will see it as *"SPAM in a can"* and move on. Such "bait and switch" tactics frequently turn off people with little free time to waste.

Many readers will also move on if they have to scroll down farther than two pages of their browser, or even one. That page is critical to the sale of your book and you must make sure the viewer always sees the cover first. The best rule of thumb is to *keep it simple.* When you are selling a book the only thing on that page should be something about it and the cover. You can also add reviews, anecdotes about the book's development, and so on, on a separate page, but again do not bombard the viewer with too much information all at once.

Do not buy a domain name and then index it to another site, because some search engines will not acknowledge the URL or reject it altogether. On search engines like *Google,* redirecting a site to another site is considered a **no-no**. The index page of your site is where the crawler robot will look, so a URL gripper to redirect is useless.

If you can, the index page of the second site can be a subfolder in the main site's list. Then all related pages can be linked to that one page. You can also speed up the listing process by submitting a sitemap page, or register with the search engine and then list your domain name with the URL of your index page.

In my case I use the index page to present my books, links to their individual pages and also to the buy buttons I use to sell them. Secondary pages are only for those buyers who want more information so I place a larger image on that page, and to make it even more attractive. But above all, the books should be the primary elements on the front page. A blog or biographical information should go on a separate page.

A few search engines will give you a special *meta tag* to put in your coding so that the link will be picked up more quickly, because the robot crawler can take months to find your site and add it to their list. The tag is essential for this.

Still another way is to look at your email address profile and see if you can add links there. The use of an automatic signature at the bottom of your email messages can accommodate a link to your site. Use it for all your emails so that you can maximize your reach to outside consumers.

If you are not sure about the rules, each domain host has a *help module* to look at in order to maximize your site's search position.

Take a look at any bookseller's site. The American Booksellers' Association, or *indiebound.org*, will have a whole list of sites which show how they set up their pages. They are uniform in that they display their contact information on their front pages along with their posted events and also links to their books for sale. On some of them they also post pictures of their physical bookstores.

The **FAQ** or **About Us** page is where you put your author biography, your publicity photo(s) and something about your publisher or your mission. Your FAQ page will assure your readers of the facts about your book or your identity, and also what kind of books you write and sell. Here you can also include other profile information.

If *you* are the publisher, you include that information as well as contact points including your email address and/or alternate email addresses if you want to. If you think you can handle the traffic include your phone number, but I would not advise it because more and more telephone marketers can and will use it to call you in the middle of the night. Your best option is to list your number on the national *do not call* list, but many unscrupulous marketers ignore that.

I don't post my phone number anywhere, or as a string of zeroes. I don't think it is anyone's business to know what my phone number is on the internet. I post my main email address, so there is no urgency which requires calling me.

Here is where you can also make specific disclaimers about the content of your books, too. There is an unwritten rule in the publishing world which says that if your book contains profanity or sexually explicit content, you should declare this so there is no ambiguity. If you do not you tacitly invite all responsibility for the ire of a parent who may find the book obscene or pornographic.

The First Amendment of the Constitution (U.S.) is your only refuge, and even then the law is not on your side. While most sites like Google include a childproof filter, pornography is considered a prosecutable offense especially when it is sold to minors. Sites which market pornography are shut down every day, so if you write this kind of book be prepared to take the heat for it.

I do not make the rules, so do not blame me if it happens. I am telling you this now so you can know what to do to stay out of trouble. Other countries will have their own rules regarding porn so make sure your butt is covered before you proceed.

If you have crafted a really great story which can stand on its own without all the heavy breathing, cut the stuff out and sell it that way. Your porn, once sanitized, may turn out to be a literary diamond in the rough. A book geared toward a more general audience will sell more copies than a book geared toward a specific niche market.

In my case I actually devote a whole page to links, events and other features which are placed there for the convenience of my site's visitors. Recently, however, I have discovered that exchanging reciprocal links actually interferes with my commerce with visitors. They may click on a link which will take them elsewhere, and the sale becomes lost at that point. It is best that you concentrate only on creating an easy hierarchy which keeps the reader interested and on track.

You can also copy snippets of Javascript as needed. The script's code may not be recognized on some browsers, but to save time you can copy the source coding for any order page you find which matches your needs and change it. But be careful to change all of the links and references to the parent site or you will end up with a 504 message on your web browser; or your page will load with errors noted, in which case it will not work.

If you still feel that you are totally net illiterate or are easily confused, you can always hire someone to code and set up the site for you. There is no shame in asking for help. Some people are not math or computer savvy to save their lives, while others think it's a breeze to sit there and code. There are many web sites and services available to help you through the rough spots, so do not let doubt stop you from achieving your goal.

The **Product Page**, (see front page) usually the book's cover, description or short blurb, product details, preview and price; and relevent buy buttons or link to an order form or shopping cart. You can include links to your other books if you choose. This kind of page is especially useful when you have more than one book to sell. Following my rule, the index page is where the product overview is presented and the product page is shown as an article detailing salient elements about the book. But it is your choice how to use it.

Others set up product pages to mimic the standard listing page on most of the sites which sell books. This is the way many booksellers set up their own sites. The only difference with mine is that I have *not* added sales rankings and "suggested books" in the same genre. These are superfluous and detract from the presentation of my own books.

These two kinds of pages are critical to the presentation of your site and must be consistent with every other product page on it. It is not good to make these pages a different color from your front page, or customers will lose interest or even get lost. If you are not sure about this, the standard white or cream background with a black font is sufficient for your needs. The color scheme I have chosen makes my site comfortable to look at and read.

To save time and effort for a site visitor, I tag my site links with the code: *target="self"*, which will create a popup window to look at. You do not need Javascript for this. A standard size window will appear containing the product image or page as needed.

The **Order Form.** You can create a good order form using *HTML, UTF-8*, or *BBcode* which can be sent directly to your email address, or to the address of your shopping cart or service. One can embed this form in the contact page for this with the tag:
<form action="mailto:your-contact-name@your-site or other contact-point.com" method="post" enctype="text/plain"> where you can include checkboxes for selections, prices, the shipping and handling charges, and so on; enclosed inside the tag **</form>**. This is especially useful instead of creating a form using the suffix *cgi* or *php*. You can create tables within these form tags to organize its appearance on the page. The *form* tag does not separate the form from the body of the page. The text and buttons within determine how you will receive the information from the customer. You can even include a text box there the customer can make special requests or modify the order.

The order form can also contain the **Terms of Sale**, the rules under which you will sell your book.

You can look up "order form templates" in your favorite search engine and download a form already made. All you have to do is modify the code to fit your needs.

How to Get Paid: There are various sites which specialize exclusively in payment processing, among which are *PayPal, Clickbank, Intuit, Stripe,* and *PayPro*. Most ask for a monthly or yearly fee in exchange for their processing services. *Stripe* takes only 5% in commissions, and so does *Facebook*.

PayPal is free to join and free to use, but you must sign up for a premier or business account first, and to speed up the process you must have either a bank account or credit card, or both, on file with them. I started with a personal account which kept getting "upgraded" every year when I used to use eBay to sell products. Since then *PayPal* had evolved into a full service site for me.

However, *PayPal* has modeled itself into a banking site in the last few months. This means they will dun you to take out a loan to conduct your business and also will transfer all money in the account to your bank rather than hang on to it. This is a double edged sword in terms of using them as a payment processor.

If you prefer you can even create buy buttons which you can embed in your site. You can set your postage or shipping rules, create a safe buying environment for your customers and also accept credit cards. In my case I even set the buttons so that only buyers over 18 will be able to buy the books. This way I ensure that the purchase is not only legal, it is responsibly made.

Fees are assessed only when you sell the product and are paid by the buyer. They also compute your shipping charges automatically according to your preferences and can also charge sales tax according to the buyer's location. *PayPal* assures the customer that you are a secure seller and they also provide you with protection from internet scammers. This is one of the most economical ways to get paid by customers without paying a fee up front for setting up the account. The only deduction it makes is at point of sale, and that amounts to less than 3% of the gross amount.

In the next section I will discuss how to market and promote your books or other product(s).

Methods of Direct Promotion

The Press Release This is one of the best and least expensive ways to get the word out about your book. The wording must be a little drier than your conventional ad. It is essentially an announcement and nothing more. But the reach of a press release will do more for you than just your web site. There are many different sites which are tailored to host press releases issued by many different companies and individuals. Some charge a fee to issue a release, but for now concentrate on finding those which allow a free release.

There is a specific set of rules to follow to draft the form of the press release. Some of these sites already have forms to help you set one up, with input boxes where you can put the information according to their format. The usual form of a press release appears like this:

The *Headline* – where you craft an appealing eyecatcher about your book or product, or a company event.

The *Summary* – a brief overview or teaser about the contents, usually the first sentence in the body of the release.

The *Body* – The complete form of the release. Here is where you inform the reader about your book. Avoid using adjectives like *"fantastic"* or phrases like *"the greatest story ever told!"* Above all, *avoid using exclamation points.* Why? Because journalists and reporters viewing these press releases will pass them by. They see bombastic prose as both amateurish and sometimes completely false, no matter if it is absolutely true.

A press release is about fact, not about what you think about your own product.

A straightforward description or blurb which includes what the book is about and where it can be found will suffice. If you have room, include a side note and a brief biography about you, the author. Devote only one paragraph to this. *Always* include your contact information in the body of the text in addition to filling out the text boxes for that purpose. In the internet age, your email address and the URL of your site should be sufficient.

You may have to edit the body text to fit their block limit. Some releases are limited to less than 5,000 characters, others 8,000 and so on. I know of one that will allow no more than 250 words. Your release will not load at all if you exceed the limit, and the form will kick it back explaining why.

In all cases, keep your prose limited only to the product you are selling or event you are promoting. Choose your words carefully so that everything you want to say is brief and to the point.

You can also issue more than one press release about other books in your library, side products and news or events, such as a book signing or your presence at a book fair or convention. Above all, this is information disseminated to the public for the public record, so your professional approach to this is essential.

The *Contact Information* – here is where you can input your site's URL, your email address and mailing address, your company name and/or your author name. This may seem redundant but it is for the release site's purposes. They will publish an external link to your site to accompany your article.

The *Book's Cover* (optional) – Often there is no place where you can embed the cover image in the body of the release, so some sites offer a way for you to upload a copy. Be sure to consult the size dimensions and the resolution of the image they will take, as well as the format. Most release sites ask for a JPG and a required size for the image. Others may require a link instead.

Always create a copy first before you resize it. *Never use the original.* You do not want to lose the permanent file, ever.

Here is a sample release should you want to issue a mail-out to newspapers and magazines. It takes the same form as the online release. It should occupy no more than a single sheet of paper.

PRESS RELEASE - For Immediate Release

ACME COMPANY ISSUES A NEW BOOK ABOUT TIN CANS

Anytown, State, USA *Date* www.acmecompany.com
Acme Company, Inc., a tin and metallurgical supply company, has just approved a new book for publication called "TIN CANS: Kicking Back 100 Years Later" by senior executive W. G. Hardy as part of its celebration of a century in business. The book is 340 pages, hard bound, and includes the history of the company, an album of photographs of the company's executives, award employees, and an overview of products it has developed and produced in that time. It will be released on (*Date*) to distribution worldwide with a list price of $29.95.

About the author: W. G. Hardy has been the vice president in charge of production for ten years and has a broad knowledge of metallurgical and tin refining processes. "TIN CANS: Kicking Back 100 Years Later" is one of three books he has written on behalf of the company. This year he will receive the Tin Man Award for his fidelity and consistent service to Acme Company.

[Here you would insert a quotation or two from the author about why he wrote the book.]

For more information, contact Helga Tinson at Acme Company. (address, phone number or email address, and repeat the URL here).

You see that it is short and devoid of exclamations and other colorful prose. It simply describes the title of the book, the number of pages and how it is being published, something about the author and when it will be distributed. This will draw attention from journalists and reporters to the book better than a slick advertising blurb filled with florid (and often inaccurate) adjectives.

Advertising - This is the place where most of your money may have to go. Once you have the product in hand (and even before that), you then have to find the most economical way to present it to your target readers. Aside from your web site and press releases, if you can get away without paying anything up front you are two steps ahead of the game. Here are some methods you can use to get your book in front of the reading public:

Flyers and **Print Media**: If you are fortunate enough to live near the site of an annual convention, book or library fair, or a bookstore row, you can also distribute flyers, bookmarks or other printed media about your book there. This can become costly. If you have the resources to afford the printing costs, it is still a good way to reach the general public. If a bookstore is friendly enough you can even leave a stack of flyers with them.

Do not expect a huge return on your investment. Most people will take the flyer but use it for something else, or throw it away without reading it later.

You can also send them by direct mail to your mailing list of friends, associates and other aquaintances. The postage and cost to print is more to bear but the risk that no one may respond is also there.

Postcards are another option. You can print your book's cover on the front side and put a short description on the back. Do not forget to leave room for your return address and your recipient's address. Postcards can be printed on index card stock; and a standard size can be from 3" x 5" up to 5" x 7" before it will exceed the postage limit. Postcards can also be generated using templates from various printing services like *vistaprint.com* and *catprint.com*.

Press kits: to reach more mass media outlets like radio and television stations, you can call them directly to pitch your book, then send them a prepared folder full of goodies like a copy of the press release, a flyer, a brief biography of you the author and related articles about the subject your book covers. This last printing option is a little more costly than a press release and involves a little more risk, but the rewards can be great if you are able to get their attention.

Bookmarks: a useful item, indeed, and can be especially helpful for selling your books. They are easy to produce and will last as long as the reader uses them to mark their place in a book. It keeps their attention on you as a bookseller. This is described in more detail in *Side Products.*

Direct email messages: sent to your target market is the most economical and time saving way to reach readers. You can take a copy of your press release, put it into text or other format, then send it to the email addresses of newspapers, magazines, social groups, associations, and even corporate entities which support your field of interest. It is not enough to issue a press release and then sit back and expect a flood of responses. You have to take a proactive approach to get the word out. You can also use mailing services like *mailchimp.com* or *constantcontact.com* to load your list of email addresses and send a simple message to all your addressees at once, saving you the time and elbow grease.

Many of these sites have online forms which you can fill out and send directly. But you may be limited in the amount of material you can upload to them. Some will allow you no more than a paragraph of space, so it is vitally important to draft a generic message as a text file, which can be trimmed if needed.

Above all, the most important parts of your message, such as the title, subject and a brief description of the book's contents and/or when it will be made available for sale, should occupy the highest priority for the content of your email message.

A word about **SPAM**. Due to the flood of email messages which are about a product or idea, many of these sites also include *spam blockers*. Do not be discouraged by this. Some site forms will insist that you fill in a box with a code which will distinguish you from what's called a *spambot*, an automated email sender which has little to no restraint when it comes to the frequency of sending the same message. If you can, include a link to a place where the recipient of the message can opt off your list.

To avoid losing contact with your target market, there is a set of rules about internet courtesy (or what is called *netiquette*) to be followed:

Avoid **sending mass mailings** which involve multiple addresses bundled into large groups. Even if you set your groups in the *Blind CC* box, the mailer bots of most email hosting services will not be able to handle the volume, and you will have a hard time sorting through your list to remove the addresses which are kicked back to you based on their particular preferences.

Some will come back as: *undeliverable, timed out, blocked,* and *unknown* or *no longer in service.* The bot will send you a long list of addresses which do not function for these reasons. I learned this the hard way. Save yourself the headache and the time.

You might be able to shave off some time in posting by creating smaller groups from these, no more than maybe ten addresses each, but sending the message to them one at a time will be most effective.

Your *subject line* should always be something about your book. In my case, I have used the headlines from my press releases. The more specific you are, the more likely it will be that the recipient will actually take a look at your message. Avoid subject lines like *"Urgent!"* *"Please Read"* and other statements which are failing attempts to get your reader's attention. Due to the number of SPAM messages which begin this way, your message may be mistaken for SPAM and will be blocked automatically and/or trashed without being read.

The *body* of your message should be free of excess material. If you can get away with a simple text message, that should be sufficient. Messages which are an exact duplicate of your web page are a no-no. Some email hosting services may not be able to support images and other bright twinkly flash ads and attachments, so remember the watch phrase is *keep it simple.* Here is where you will be seen as a serious author or publisher with a really good book to sell. Your email should be like your press release.

Avoid using large attachments. If you are tempted to do this it is a waste of your time. The format of your attachment, such as a chapter from your book or an image, may not be compatible with the recipient's browser or email service capacity. You may be able to embed something in your message body, but this too may cause problems. *You should be able to sell the book with your simple text message alone.* If you do want to send an attachment, keep the piece no bigger than 2MB to 5MB. Your hosting service will tell you how big the attachment can be.

The *frequency* of sending a promotional message can also affect your ability to reach your target audience. If you send it to your recipients once a week or daily I can safely guarantee your message will be blocked as SPAM. True, you may not want it to be seen that way, but you are playing to the sympathy of the recipient. When a recipient replies and asks you to remove them from your list, do so. There are literally *millions* of others who will pay attention. Do not stress over one or two.

Also, do not take it personally. You are competing with a vast network of competitors for their attention.

I have received polite responses from recipients who thanked me for the message rather than blocked me. If you do this you are making a friend, especially when all they do is offer you a link exchange or even express a real interest in reading your book.

Ad space: taken out or rented and placed in your local newspaper or a national magazine. Print ads can eat into your budget like a wildfire in a pine forest. It is a short term and often ephemeral part of your operating costs. If you are ambitious enough to embark on an advertising campaign of this kind you may be able to *amortize* the cost instead. More about this in the section called **Accounting For Sales and Operations.**

Each newspaper or magazine will have what is called a **rate card**, which shows the sizes of ad space available and their cost. A single ad placement is far more expensive than a series of consecutive ads. You are in essence contributing to the print cost of the whole page in an issue divided among the number of ads placed on it. The cost per ad is discounted the more times you use it. But for a magazine with a print run of 100,000 or more, this can become quite costly to an author with a limited budget. An ad space the size of a business card (2"x3") can cost $250 or more to start, *increasing* exponentially in the case of larger ads.

A print ad is also more risky for its reach. Readers of magazines and newspapers may pass over your ad, so at best you may be able to effect a subliminal message which may trigger a response later, but not immediately. And with the increasing popularity of the internet as a virtual mall and networking universe, most of your sales contacts will more likely be found there than in a magazine.

The fact is that most newspapers and magazines depend heavily on advertising revenues to keep going. We have seen major newspaper publishers file for bankruptcy because of the decline in readership and advertising. As the availability of these avenues shrink, so will your target audience. If you still want to go that route go ahead, but it is better to take advantage of the other less expensive alternatives before you.

One alternative which may get you more attention is to send a review copy of your book to the book review section of the newspaper. But even that will not guarantee you will be noticed or even reviewed. The reviewer may only be interested in mainstream literature and/or nonfiction on current topics, so your new cookbook or your latest memoir may be neglected.

There also others who will not read self-published work, period, out of a time honored policy established by the newspaper. It is not to your benefit to engage in butting heads with them. Skip over them and send your book to reviewers who will work with you.

Avoid *reviewing services* which will charge to review your book. In most cases you will not get an honest review, which is important to help you determine if your book is saleable. In my case, I belonged to an independent publishers' group which engaged in selling ad space to reach book stores and reviewers. I tried this for a year, and the reviews I got were free only after I paid $$$ to advertise this way. But reviews did not get the books sold any faster than without them.

Per click ads: Here I must talk about the newest way to promote your book, which can fast become a money pit if you are not careful. Per click advertising is where you buy ad space which is displayed on another site and depends heavily on the number of clicks received. For example, Google's *Adsense* feature allows you to buy or sell ads in the form of a patch embedded in the code of your web page. A company wanting to participate has to bid for a space in the patch. For each click on a link, the company pays a penny.

If you put up a patch to monetize your site, each click on a link pays you a penny. But this form of advertising has usually resulted in very little to no income because people will not click on the ads, period. Advertisers have talked extensively about this problem and it is not to your benefit to engage in a campaign which yields no fruit.

Shoppers may even avoid buying from you simply because your site is cluttered with ads. They do not want to be bombarded with ads from other sites. Flash animation ads are treated even worse, because they have been reported to cause epileptic seizures among those afflicted with the disease. You should avoid using ad patches altogether and make your site as clean and consumer oriented as possible. Remember that your goal is to get people to buy *your* book, not to gain income from advertising clicks.

Another new addition to the "gimme" market is Facebook's ad program, which charges a fixed amount per click for a limited number of clicks. I experimented with it once the price to promote went down to a certain amount per thousand impressions. The number of resulting clicks told me that Facebook users are not interested in "liking" or clicking on ad links.

The bill went to $100 in two weeks, when I stopped using FB ads altogether. Later I used Facebook Ads only to promote news which I felt was important to my business plan, such as the publication of my books. I spent less money by sharing the news among most of the FB groups I belong to.

Recently, auto manufacturer General Motors pulled its Facebook ads citing the same problem. When advertising is ineffectual in a certain market, it makes no difference if you are big or small.

Your other option is to establish a "Facebook page" for your product or company. Beware before you start posting. Some users have taken steps to remove advertisers' pages by clicking the "*report abuse*" button. When that happens you are the guilty party no matter how innocent your are, and you have to prove your innocence to Facebook to get it restored.

Your best option is to post your promotional material on your own feed wall or profile and share it with your target readers. If you can afford to be that social go for it. As you accumulate "like" clicks your profile will attract more interest than an ad.

Remember that Facebook users are looking for social interaction, not advertising, and your best bet for attracting readers is to sell it yourself from your own site. I belong to several Facebook groups which are geared toward books of specific genres, which means I have access to interested FB users.

Networking: in person is also a good way to polish your people skills, especially when you are going to participate or organize a book signing or other event on your own. If you are shy to begin with, this is where you test your ability to socialize with others on a less personal level than with your peers. Don't expect to sell anything, however. It is just a way to fit in.

Let me warn you about these kinds of gatherings, however. Use them to promote your latest book, but if you are in the process of writing or editing one, they can be a waste of useful production time. For example, I once attended a "book talk" event, which turned out to be a bar hop. The noise in that room was so loud that it was like standing next to a jet plane about to take off. I could not engage in conversations with real publishers or agents. Most of the people there were there to drink and little else.

Talk to corporations about sponsorships and gift promotions. Your book may be about something the corporation may find to be an aid to its marketing or selling model. The company can make your book a tie-in gift with the purchase of its products, or as a free promotional give away. If you nail one of these contracts you will make a lot of money from just one purchase.

Participate in a book fair. This is the best way to get your book seen in the flesh by a wide market of shoppers. The biggest book convention I know of is *Book Expo America*, which is a wholesaler and industry show. You may be able to get in on this by joining the Jenkins Group *Combined Exhibit*. But you have to pay a membership fee per year and also a fee to include your book on their shelves. This fee applies for each title you want to present.

As an alternative, the Independent and Small Publishers Association West and the Independent Book Publishers Association (IBPA) will allow you to display your books with theirs on their display space. But you have to join their group first and also pay a proportionate amount of the display charges. They provide an online newsletter which you can subscribe to.

Another is the *Los Angeles Times Book Fair*, which is held on the campus of USC (University of Southern California). The cost of a booth is a little beyond most authors' pocketbooks, and once you are there you will be competing with both traditional and small press publishers, as well as other self-published authors. But if you can afford it do not pass up the opportunity to visit. Even if you do not have a booth you may be able to sell your book, participate in the panel discussions and book signings, and you can pass out postcards, bookmarks and other media there, too. It is free to get in.

If you cannot afford to travel you should look up book fairs and festivals in your local area. If there are none, widen your search to include swap meets and craft festivals. People there are just as likely to buy your books as at the other places I mentioned. It may entail a bit more investment from your pocketbook, but it is an opportunity to sell more books than you do online. You also have the opportunity to become a member of your local community and to become well known there.

The **American Library Association** presents a list of book fairs on their site but these are mostly for sale of used books for dimes to the dollar. They are useful for circulating flyers but not for selling new books. However, if you are specializing in selling used books along with your new books, it is also an economical way to promote your books or to unload books you no longer want to keep. These are also good places to pass the word about books you are working on.

Sell at a media or literary convention. There are a whole bunch of comic book and media conventions presented in every major city on the planet every year. One of these is the largest media and comic book convention in the United States, called *Comic-Con International.*

Born in 1973 as a small local convention held in a San Diego hotel, it rapidly grew beyond its borders every year since, until some of the corporate publishers of comic books and media recognized its worth as a promotional venue and sponsored its move into the San Diego Convention Center.

For 5 days in mid July or August, thousands of people visit and explore the dealers' room to spend money on books, comic books, games and videos for a fee. Many books and comic books have seen their debuts there and sold very successfully.

While their exhibit space fees are exhorbitant, if you can talk to a seller planning to exhibit there you might be able to share the fees and participate in selling at a booth. Groups of authors or sellers have banded together to do this before, and one advantage is that you will get to see some of the convention yourself while being able to sell your books.

In 2012 over 500,000 people attended over 5 days. Recently there has been talk that the con directors are thinking of splitting into two forms, but so far nothing has been announced.

Another L.A. convention, called **Wondercon**, made a move from San Francisco to Anaheim and took off. It became nearly as big as **Comic Con**. But again, there is little chance of competing unless you have the money to finance a booth.

A lot of the smaller and more local science fiction, fantasy, horror and/or mystery conventions are hosted by fan clubs and nonprofit associations, and are mostly composed of readers and media lovers. They started out interested in reading books and went on to embrace films and television shows in those particular genres. But all are interested in good writing and will welcome your participation.

It is actually more economical to hire a booth at one of these than at one of the larger conventions, and there is less chance that you will be swallowed up or shoved into the background by the corporate media blitz. If you have friends who have a similar interest you can also treat it as a weekend party. Some of these shows actually label themselves "relaxicons", but their dealers' rooms are still filled with wonders and delights, from jewelry to rare books to handmade gifts and other items.

There are sellers there who even travel from convention to convention like gypsies, and make a good living from their work. If you are the adventurous sort you might find this a good way to pay your bills while writing.

There are larger regional conventions such as **Westercon** (Western US), **Boskone** (Boston), **Noreascon**, **Norwescon** and **Dragon Con** (Atlanta). The *Worldcon* is the largest and most oriented convention geared for readers and writers; held in a different major city each year. There are also conventions for specific subgenres like the *World Fantasy Convention* and the *World Horror Convention.* Other conventions which are more dedicated to media include *Japan Expo, Anime Expo*, and *Wizard World* (for gamers and game developers). If your product is something other than a book you might find it worth your while to explore some or all of these and learn what it takes to sell there.

If you are an author of children's books, you can still sell your books at one or all of these, or at specialty shows devoted to children. Fans have children, and some of them are children who never grew up. The "Peter Pan Syndrome" is common among the fan community, and many appreciate the innocence and fun of a good children's book. Here you can find afficionados of specific books by authors like Dr. Seuss, C.S. Lewis, H. L. Baum and others. Do not be afraid to try one out.

You can also set up to sell books at "celebrity autograph" shows. There is one I used to go to where movie and television stars set up tables to sell their autographed photos and meet their fans. The rest of the convention area was packed end to end by sellers of books, collectibles and comic books, as well as television and film memorabilia.

The possibilities are endless when it comes to spending a little money and setting yourself up to sell your own product. It is also a way to make extra cash to fund your next project.

Bookstore signings and **reading events**: Approach the manager of a bookstore and convince him to arrange a signing. Most will be happy to, since this gives them an opportunity to bring in more customers and sell books other than yours. But you will have to bear some of the promotional costs as well as the cost of the unsold books. This means that basically you must be prepared to pay for advertising and be ready to deal with anything else.

Reserve space for a reading in a library. You should include a lecture in your program. Even if you feel you are not good at public speaking here is your chance to learn how to get over your stage fright and engage an audience. You can sign and sell your book there as long as you allow for a portion of the proceeds to be donated to the branch which hosts your signing. The cost of the donation can be taken on your tax return.

I remember reading a question from one author in a forum one day, who asked if it was alright to price the books higher in order to collect the donation. I must remind you **not** to do this. If the price of the book is printed on the back cover, any buyer will question why you are charging more. It will also prevent you from making any sales at all.

You must strike a balance between being reasonable and being greedy, but not on the backs of the buyers. Above all, you must be charitable also, and if it achieves the goal of getting your books out there it is the best way to show that you care.

Arrange to give a reading in a cafe with a bookstore, or a nightclub which specializes in wine and prose.

These are all good ways to sell your book in a public setting which will concentrate your reader base in one spot. Do not be disappointed if you do not succeed the first time. Your persistence and perseverence will help you to achieve your goal.

The Promotional Video - If you are a complete novice at this here is where I can help you make a simple video that will do more to help you market your book than anything else you might do. The *Press Release* is effective, but the *video* has more reach. You can make it as exciting and attention grabbing as the best movie trailer on the planet. The better you make it, the more people will be inclined to watch it, and often video sharing is a better way to spread the word about your book or product than you might think.

You can also upload an audio file of an interview or a reading by you to generate interest in the book, with pictures if possible. Once viewers are engaged with the plot, they may go on to purchase the book.

Let's face it. In this media driven world, people are more prone to pay attention to movement, colors and bright lights than to a print ad for a book. A whole generation of potential readers has grown up glued to the television set. But why is this important when you are selling a book? Because most of them are still interested in good prose despite their fascination, and you may have no other way to reach such a large population when you are publishing on a shoestring budget.

YouTube, powered by *Google*, is the most widely watched and searched video sharing site in the world. They host live action videos of important events, television episodes, movies in the public domain, commercials, trailers, political satire, comedy, cute animals doing cute things, stupid people doing stupid things, and a whole variety of other presentations ranging in length from ten seconds to twenty minutes long.

Once the video is uploaded half of your marketing work will be done for you. Depending on the subject of your book, the number of views generated by your video can also serve as a barometer of interest in your book or its subject. The longer it remains up, the more views there will be. You can even attract ratings and comments which will help you to determine if it is reaching the right audience. Leave it up long enough and it may even make the front page of the site, though that has not happened even for best sellers. If you are a publisher as well as an author, this is how you can establish your professional image or marketing brand for the public.

The most important segments which must be included for the video to be of some use are a short description or bit of teaser prose, the cover of the book, where it can be bought and where information for it can be found. By then you should have already bought a domain and created a site for your book or publishing company where viewers could go to see it, or at least the places where your book is available for sale.

You do not need music, but for sites viewed by media hungry viewers, music is an added bonus. But *be careful* with this. You cannot upload videos containing current or complete pop music or you would be subject to copyright conflicts and possible prosecution by the content owners.

You can use edited music from free players or music in the public domain. If you have a friend who can cobble some original music together for you, that is even better.

You should keep up your video presence constantly, so that people will not forget about it You are competing with thousands of other people all vying for the viewer's attention at the same time. In the explosion of videos being uploaded everyday, you need to stay out front like a salmon swimming upstream. Never look back.

YouTube and other video sharing sites will accept uploads in a variety of formats (see their FAQ to learn what they are).

Book trailers should always be short, sweet and to the point. I have found that a simple slideshow of art and phrases accompanied by music timed to match can be assembled with a few hours of labor, and a little artistic flair I have been able to obtain software which enables me to create mpg4 files in higher quality than I used to. The higher the definition, the more likely viewers will stay to watch.

My first video was as long as three minutes. My latest are as short as forty five seconds. Remember that viewers have shorter attention spans than readers, so it is vitally important to engage their attention and keep it. I have also seen many excellent book videos assembled from live action clips and inserted slides.

You may have better luck if you have friends who are willing to act out scenes from your book; or if you have the money you can hire someone to produce one for you.

Among all the benefits of producing a video is the fun you can have making it. It is also advantageous to make different types and lengths of videos about your book. Remember that *variety is the spice of life*. You may also discover a hidden talent you did not know you had.

Let us start with the basics: a *simple slideshow* assembled into a video clip. The image slides can be made on Adobe Photoshop or any other standard image processing software. You should look to invest in something which will help you produce the best quality images possible because the images in your books will stand the same rigorous test. You want to save money while doing this, so go slow until you have had enough practice to move to more advanced versions.

Here is a sample of one of my own slides. It is 1920 x 1080 pixels at 150 dpi (dots per inch) rendered in grayscale, using a typeface which is commonly known as Viking Normal. The actual color of the lettering is bright scarlet but I show it here as light grey. The resolution really makes little difference in the aspect ratio of the image as long as the dimensions remain the same. But if you want a clear image and have red stand out more, the higher the resolution the better.

ⵁANTELLUS
www.antellus.com

The smallest size can be 320 x 240 at 72 dpi, but if people want to blow it up the picture will become grainy and pixilated. The size I chose is the finer grade. Lately, since many tablets and smart phones are set up at an even higher resolution, I have started creating videos geared toward smart phones and tablets.

Different image processors will interpret the data for the image differently, and various sites will present colors differently. **Vimeo**, for example, shows the videos as clear as crystal. **YouTube** shows them slightly blurry and the red tends to fade out or pixilate on a black background; though they have recently improved their presentation so that the red does not fade or blur quite as much. Also, your choice of screen resolution can clear up these problems.

You can use any color and any photo background or lettering you like. If you are not sure the image is sharp enough, I would recommend you sharpen the image before you save it. To avoid glare from white lettering I use light grey against black or some other dark color like oxblood or midnight blue. You should not create slides which will make the viewer uncomfortable when looking at it. The contrast alone can be murder on the optic nerves.

Here is where you can get creative. Give out hints or key features of the story, but do not tell the whole story. Leave something for the reader to crave, or you will not keep their interest for long. For example, in the book video for my fiction books, I added slides of the pictures I had inserted in the books. I set them to music which marched to the pace of the pictures, so that people could enjoy it more as they could see what they are getting for their purchase. It can also be a form of mobile portfolio if you happen to have any illustration or artistic skill.

I center the image of the cover on a black or dark colored background as large as I can. I used to leave a margin of 10 pixels top and bottom, but that only reduces the image of the cover, so I started putting the cover flush left with black on both sides.

Then you will need another slide to show where the book can be found, which includes the *URL of your web site* and/or which online sellers or bookstores are selling it for you. In my case I have managed to combine both on one slide, so that the cover and the information about it are seen at once.

If you have written a series of books in a particular genre, you can blend all the covers together on one video and save yourself the time it takes to make one for each. Just be sure to leave enough time for the images to sink into the viewer's memory, and be sure to time the book cover slide so that slow readers can read what it on it.

A sample of a book slide.

The **end slide**. This can be a plain black slide or a *thank you for your attention* slide. The end slide is not necessary but it projects a more friendly attitude on your part if you thank your audience for their attention. The black slide enables you to end your presentation cleanly with a fade to black, which signals the video's end. If you are working on a project made by a group, you can include a slide presenting the credits due for their collaboration, music credit, and so on between the book slide and the end slide.

I have seen videos which begin and end as a series of images and nothing more; and some are so short one cannot get a real sense of what they are actually about. You are free to use your own judgment but artistic license or aesthetics may also drive your ability to reach your target audience.

Once you assemble the image slides and arrange them in the order you want, you will need an image processor to put them together. I use *Roxio Media Creator NXT6*. It is reasonably user friendly and can do all the things you want, from creating a sound or video file to recording and burning CDs, DVDs and the like.

When you import your images to the storyboard, you can insert fade transitions where you want them. You can then set the times for these images to display, how long you want the effects to last, and you can also set the timing of the whole storyboard to music. There is an automatic button for this, but I have a musical background so I prefer to time the slides and transitions myself.

When you have finished and saved your production you output the storyboard to the video converter, which helps you create the finished product. The menu of selections is quite extensive, and you can create your output based on the size of slides you used. Once you are satisfied with the result, you finish and save the video. The default format is usually *.wmv*. The latest version allows you to save the file as any other video and film format available, including iPad and generic formats *.mpg2*, *.mpg4*, and *.achv*. The best resolution of output is 60px.

The Roxio also contains a *Sound Editor*. This is eminently useful if you want to insert a narration track, or narration and background music mixed together, into the production. When you do this you have the added benefit of reaching many more viewers with your presentation, as many of them prefer to see the whole package all at once. I have been lucky enough to find music which not only matches the theme of my books, I can time the slides to match the music. This is your opportunity to shine as a creative person.

The slideshow format is the simplest to make, but if you want to do more, you can also produce animated videos using slides, or assemble video clips and splice them together. Other processing software like Adobe Premiere 16 works in a similar fashion. It is your choice which will help you create an effective trailer.

The main point here is that you can advertise your book this way for little to no cost, so use all the resources at your disposal. Later, as you earn more from the sale of your book you can reinvest a small amount for more professional services. You can hire someone to perform voice narration for the sound file, or rent studio time to make one yourself. The possibilities and opportunities are endless.

Side Products: Along with your book you can also produce a whole raft of what are called *side* or *tie-in products*. They can come in the form of ebooks, audiobooks, books of art inspired by the book, bookmarks in the theme of the book or products based on the book, like video games, videos, and also tee-shirts and other tangible gift products. If you are as proud of your finished work as you should be, you will attract more interest in your book if you also offer one or more of these for sale alongside.

Create an audiobook: This product has been around since sound was recordable. Though not popular for the conventional music lover, book readings have been made on wax cylinders, vinyl records, magnetic tape, casettes, and now through software and the use of professional readers that use text to speech software. Audiobooks are valuable for education of the vision impaired and as a hands-free method of enjoying a book if you are too busy to sit down and page through.

Audiobooks are usually considered to be *side products* of the actual books but they have gained popularity in the last few years with the development of iPod and other listening devices. People can and do make money producing and selling them, so you should look into making your book into an audiobook as a matter of course. Lately audio plays performed by celebrities have become very popular, and frees the listener to experience the book hands free.

Produce an *art book* or a *calendar*. Fantasy art can be a useful marketing tool. For distribution I recommend *Bud's Art Books*, which markets and sells art books from everywhere and by anyone. There are other services which specialize in these kinds of products. If your self-help publisher has the facility to create them for you, you have to use the same production model as you would with a book. Study the FAQ to help you set up the files or for templates which will help you.

A note about art books: you are also limited by your printer's offering of trim sizes and what formats they will produce. A printed color art book costs more per page to print than a regular black & white book. Keep that in mind when planning one.

Here is the cover for a portfolio book I published myself:

This was formatted as 8.5" x 11", black & white/grayscale interior with a color cover. It was just published in 2019.

Bookmarks: can be produced for sale or to give away just by using your word processor and inserting images, then printing them out on card stock. If you want to sell them you could invest in a laminator. If you are really ambitious you can hire a printing company to make them up for you. All you have to do is set up your bookmark image and upload it to them.

But be careful that you do not spend too much money on this, because it is only an advertising and promotional product. Some bookmark designers get an ISBN or UPC for each design for resale in book and gift shops, however these are not necessary when you are selling them directly from your site. Just make sure you post a copyright for each design somewhere on the bookmark itself.

If you are not inclined to invest the time and effort I would recommend that you instead choose from a group of suppliers which produce these already, like *vistaprint.com* or *catprint.com*; so you can have a supply of premade designs for sale on your site.

Offer a line of **tee-shirts, mugs,** and **bill caps** with your logo or cover design on them. It is another way to make money off your idea, though there is an investment to be made in order to profit. You can produce them for company employees, promotional giveaways or even for direct sale.

CafePress is supposed to be a handy service for this but they are a little pricey, taking as much as 85% of the retail price as a commission. In essence, you are buying the product as close to retail as possible for them, which is great if you are promoting your brand but lousy if you want to sell the product for a decent profit margin.

When you upload your logo to them the uploader will show you how it looks on various products, called *blanks*. All you have to do is select the product you want to sell, and they will pay you a small commission for the sale of each; usually no more than about a dollar per shirt, mug or bill cap.

Their file organization is also a little complex so I would advise you start with one design before you wade in. Your design may also get lost among the millions of other designs presented on the site if you do not place it in the right category.

Or, you can hire a local tee-shirt printer to make them for you. The same with mugs or bill caps. A really hot commodity used to be products with mechanized embroidery, but it is cheaper to use screenprinting instead. You will have to do a little research to find the best price for this, and be sure that you find a printer that uses washable dyes for your products.

I used to pass by a novelty printer in the mall who produced iron-on stencils and printed custom tee-shirts, bill caps, baby clothes and so on for customers as singles or as a series. Their stencils were of very good quality inks so the designs lasted longer. I know because I bought one for myself. I still have it after 20 years of wear.

You can even print them yourself by buying the right inks, dyes or paints and learning the printscreen process. It is both messy and smelly (some of the chemicals are toxic if not used properly) but if you are not bothered by that you can also generate a decent bit of income from this industry and you can even print other people's custom designs.

I have seen people selling these products directly at trade shows, business conventions and book or product fairs as well as genre conventions, so if you can find a seller you can consign your design to them and they will pay you for the sales.

But be careful. There are copyright issues with regard to media-based designs. Comic book heroes are consistent sellers at comic book conventions but they are already copyright protected. Designs like dragons and wizards, unicorns, mermaids, handsome knights and other generic images, may have a better time selling than a tee-shirt for a specific book.

There are also tee-shirt collectors who will crave nothing but media tie-ins from television shows and books which have achieved only current popularity. The market value of a tee-shirt will go down as the popularity of the subject wanes.

You can also sell the rights to produce a *video game* based on the premise of your book. Some authors are able to do both, or create their own, but only under the right circumstances. You are not likely to get this far if your book does not appeal to the people who play these games, but it never hurts to try to attract the interest of gaming developers. The gaming industry carries the opportunity to earn more for your idea than just the book itself.

The DOs and DON'Ts of Marketing

Along with all the other methods you can use to reach your readers, there are also some things you should do and avoid whenever possible. As a self-publisher your personal image is just as important as the books and other materials you are trying to sell.

Do keep your web site updated as often as possible. Each new thing you learn about projecting your public persona as an author and/or publisher should be reflected on the appearance of your site. Updates are a way to show that you are willing to interact with your customers. I update my site as frequently as once a week depending on the amount of changes I have to make. If you also maintain a blog page, keep your news short and interesting but to the point. I have seen sites which have not been changed or updated in over a year, and they look as if little thought was put into them. Some are "parked" on free space but there is nothing there to attract the reader beyond a list of other sites. I have also seen sites which list other sites, which in turn list still more sites. These will do nothing to promote or sell your book.

Do as much cross promotion as you can through link exchanges, or offer advertising space on your site. if you are offered a chance to participate in an ad for publication, here is a way you can save money. But avoid cross promotions or networking sites which require that you pay a fee to join in. Some of these sites may boast of huge successes but may not be telling the truth. There is *no guarantee* that your participation will get you the recognition or sales you hoped for. Similarly, readers may be turned off by the ads you post on your site. Popups are annoying.

Do not use sites willing to list and sell your book for you but offer no more than a credit in exchange, which you can only redeem by selecting another book from their list. I participated in one of these sites but found that a year later they were shut down for lack of the proper web site certification and I lost the $2.00 I earned there.

Do join as many groups and associations that you can afford to which relate directly or indirectly to your chosen genre. The more of these accept your membership, the more likely your name will be recognized among their member readers. Name recognition will generally lead to more contacts and more sales.

Do devote some of your time to looking for new places to list or publicize your book. The search engines contain literally thousands of sites where you can. All it takes a little time and dedication.

Do not get sucked into too many *community forums* or *your Facebook feed*. Not only is this a way to get the word out about your book, it also endangers your productivity time, so posting on a forum can become a double edged sword. Learn to keep your comments short and to the point so that you can say what you want to without devoting too much time to the process.

True, these are helpful in giving you information, but there is the temptation to get into discussions you might not enjoy, or which may do more to hurt your reputation as an author than to help it.

I have to warn you that there are people who do nothing but troll these forums looking for people to criticize harshly for the sake of criticism alone. I call them *net sharks*. They are more concerned with seeing their own words in print than in the subject or topic itself. Criticizing others makes them feel important at the expense of someone else. Do not be baited into an argument with these people. It is not only a waste of time, it is a vexation to your spirit. This toxic environment can be harmful to your self-esteem and has no practical value or benefit to you.

Many people merely lurk without making a comment and take what they can from the more positive aspects, which is what you should do also. Or better still, *work on finishing your book* or start a new one, and read only as much as keeps you up to date on book trends or publishing news.

Do not blog too much. Not only is blogging a way to get the word out about your book, it also endangers your productivity time. I read a recent article about one author who got so mired in blogging that he stopped writing books altogether, much to the disappointment of his publisher. He even canceled the submission of his next book. He had become so addicted to the process that he could not extricate himself.

If you can, use blogging only for promotion or thoughts related to writing and researching your latest project. Remember that people who like to read blogs do not read books, and vice versa, so keep blogging as the last thing on your list to do for the day.

Do not use profanity or bombastic statements when discussing a topic in any venue, especially your blog. Your ability to be taken seriously as an author often depends entirely on your *netiquette*. The use of profanity in your personal life may be perfectly okay in a social or familiar setting, but many people will skip a web site which posts comments like these, and *you will be seen as unprofessional*. Again, I do not make the rules. It is up to you to change your outlook and your approach on your own.

Do not waste your time with outside activities which eat into your writing or production time. Very often, friends and family demand a great deal of your time without understanding what it takes to write a book. It is just as much a job as any other, even if you are not earning a steady salary, and you invest just as much energy and emotional commitment to the task. I

If you become embroiled in negative family issues it can take a long time for you to get back into the game zone, so it is to your benefit to set down some rules which will help you avoid them or you will be sucked into situations which will damage your productivity and emotional well-being. Often all it takes is a little assertiveness, such as saying, "while this door is closed I am working, so I do not want to be disturbed unless the world is coming to an end." Then follow it up by sticking a "do not disturb" sign on your doorknob.

Do plan your schedule to avoid needless stress. Make time for regular meals, morning mail, excercise, family and friends, education, entertainment, and most important, *sleep*. Set aside a specific block of time for writing and stick to it. There is nothing in marketing or promoting your work which should make you lose any sleep, and nothing which cannot be put off to the next day unless it is subject to a specific deadline. Your marketing time should occupy no more than 10% of your day.

A word about deadlines: There is no such thing as a deadline. If you are writing a book and you have imposed a deadline for the publication of your book, abandon the deadline. First of all, writing is a process, and the benefits lie in the journey, not the destination. If you are lucky enough to get an agent and that agent finds you a publisher, fine; but do not assume that you can write a book for them as if it is a book report. It worked in high school, but it will not work as part of your creative process.

The best way to produce the highest quality book is to finish it. Worrying about deadlines is a procrastination machine. It will eat into your creative juices and inhibit you from producing your best work. I have seen many writers fail at producing a book because of the pressure most publishers impose on their schedules.

Remember, writing is your skill at telling a good story. But don't take too long at crafting your masterpiece. Stop when you feel you are at a good place, then edit and polish as necessary. That way, anxiety will not hamstring you. Take a deep breath and then hand off the finished piece to your publisher. If by chance you feel it could be better, devote some time on rewriting the finished manuscript for later revision or as another book.

In the next section, you will learn about how to cost and price your book or product.

HOW TO PRICE AND SELL YOUR BOOK

Calculate Your Unit Cost of Production

Along with all the advertising and promotion you should do for your book, the price of the book is important to sales and a lower price makes it more attractive to bargain seekers. The fact is that most people want something for nothing, or as near to it as will satisfy their needs. You need to break through that mentality by offering your book or product for as little as possible without undercutting your profit margin, otherwise you will not gain anything from the sale yourself.

First of all, I must explain this to you so you understand what the retail, or list price, is. Many self-publishing authors seeking to sell their book on the open marketplace are easily confused by the concept of the retail price.

The **SUGGESTED RETAIL or *LIST PRICE* of a book or product is the *maximum* a seller may charge for the book NEW. It is the price at which <u>Books in Print</u> records the value of the book at the retail level. It is NOT the price at which the book *must* always sell. The** list price is often set as the *perceived value* of the book on the marketplace.

Many sellers can and do discount the retail price of the book in order to drive sales. They are in competition with each other, and to sell the book they must set a price lower than the list price to achieve a sale. At the retail level, this price is a benchmark. Some bookstores, like Powell's Books, do sell the book at this price. That is their choice. It is not etched in stone.

Once the book becomes available as *used* or *out of print*, any seller can offer the book for whatever he wants for it, if he can find a buyer at the price he sets. If not, he will consistently lower the price to the level at which someone will accept it and buy. That is simple economics at work. You have no control over this. Once the book is bought from you that is it. The single copy sold is fair game.

The price you plan to list has to match what you want to earn minus the costs of sales as well as the cost of production. You do not want it to be too high or too low. That's right; there are **two** components to costing your book. To that end, here are some concepts for you to absorb.

Costs of production: the actual costs to print your book. Most self-help publishing services present you with a list of the trim sizes for a book and what it costs to print based on a minimum amount, called the *base cost*. This is the cost to print within a range of pages, usually between 48 and 108 pages, then on a sliding scale upward to a maximum number. Here are some comparisons:

Lulu charges $4.53 + 2 cents per page for a 100 page paperback book. This their unit price for setup and printing. The price per page is for the paper and ink. So the cost to print would be $6.53. Shipping is extra.

KDP charges $3.66 for the same book. Shipping is extra.

Lightning Source charges $2.52 for the same book shipped direct to you for resale. For wholesale orders, the cost goes down to $.90 per book + $.015 per page. So for the same book the cost to print goes down to $2.25. Shipping is extra.

With these printers, a large book with illustrations will cost more to print. Each company's book fees are based on its *economy of scale*; that is, their own costs of materials, labor and other costs to produce the book for you. Keep this in mind because you will be doing the same thing yourself.

Costs of Sales: all other costs associated with the sale of your book, including the the commission charged by your online seller, as well as the amount you want to earn on each book sold. This is why it is vitally important that you *realize* or calculate all your costs in order to determine what price to charge and the amount of profit or royalty you want or expect from each sale. You also have to take into account the wholesale discount if you decide to sell the book through any distribution source to booksellers.

The standard *wholesale* discount on the list price of the book is a *minimum* of 55%. Do not be afraid of this number. If you keep in mind that your royalty amount is part of the remainder, you will do just fine. You might set the discount at just 50%, and that might be okay with some booksellers, but the larger number is the amount most major book chains expect to receive to buy your book for resale. You are less likely to sell a book for resale if you adjust it any lower. Some online booksellers, like Amazon, take 60 to 65%. I kid you not.

We combine all of these items into one number:

Unit Cost = Costs of Production + Costs of Sales

The equation used to determine the list price will prevent you from charging too much or too little for a book.

List Price = Unit Cost x 1.55 - or - Unit Cost / .45

With some self-publishing services the price can get absurdly high and out of step with similar books on the larger market. For example, say you want to earn $3.00 for every book sold. This is a safe amount to ask for, because as you increase the royalty amount the list price will also incease; so do not let greed sway your decision at this point.

For example, *Lulu* takes your **unit cost of production** and doubles it. This is a process called **keystoning**, a time honored process which is not confined to book sales. Department stores and boutiques also use it, which is why they can have so many sales which offer deep discounts and also why they should not. But what this does is balloon your *list price* out of your selling market. If you allow them to list your book anywhere at the price they set, you will never sell your books. However, retailers like *Amazon* will take that list price and offer a deep discount to its customers regardless of the cost. That is how they make the book more attractive to buy from them.

Lulu normally charges about $4.53 + $.02 per page. For a 100 page book costing $6.53 ($4.53 + $2.00) your list price would normally be around $16.26, or **[($4.53 + $2.00) x 2] + $3.00.** *Lulu* typically begins your calculation for a list price by offering you $4.00 per book as a "royalty". But here is what *Lulu* does next. It will take 20% commission from the royalty amount, not the list price. So your calculation for the list price must take that into account.

Unit cost = $6.53 + (20% of $3.00) = $7.13
List price = (2 x $7.13) + $3.00 = $17.26

In the book world you must always round UP to the nearest dollar less five cents or less a penny, so your book's list price can be **$17.95** or **$17.99**. The standard for the list price from 1 to 5 cents less than the next higher dollar can be the difference between the type of book being sold. This becomes the **perceived value** of the book on the marketplace.

People will focus on the dollar part of the price first, and the extra 95 or 99 cents is typically ignored despite the fact that they are actually paying a dollar more than what they see.

Trade paperbacks are typically sold at 5 cents less; while the smaller or what are called mass market paperbacks are sold at 1 cent less. The markdown reflects your economy of scale when it comes to pricing the book, and the 5 cent cut is considered better than the 1 cent cut. The same applies to hardback books.

But when you let Lulu calculate it for you, they do this:

List price = 2 x ($7.13 + $3.00) = $20.26

The list price is then rounded up to **$20.95** or **$20.99**. But here is the deal with *Lulu*: **you would still get only $2.40 from the sale of each book.** Lulu earns 100% profit on the sale of your book and recovers all its costs, including the cost of paying you a royalty. And it never discounts the list price of the book in their online marketplace. If you get a distribution package with them, there is no guarantee of any net gain over that $3.00, and as I said before they do *not* guarantee a *return credit* to booksellers.

Their distribution packages vary. If you want to sell on Amazon, *Lulu* will be glad to attach a free ISBN to your book, but in their agreement with Amazon they must allow for a wholesale discount on the sale of the book and they insist on becoming your publisher imprint. This means the whole enchilada is recalculated by *Lulu* this way:

$$\text{List price} = \$10.13 / .40 = \$25.33$$

The 40% is Amazon's payout to Lulu. Amazon typically keeps the lion's share of the sale. It means your little 100 page book has been priced *WAY* out of proportion. When you round up, your book is even further priced out of the market. Readers will look at the number of pages and wonder why they have to pay so much for such a thin or small book.

This is why *Lulu* is very good at publishing your book and making it available to you for resale from your own store, web site or their base marketplace, but not at all good for distribution. Recently, they have also tacked on a fee on top of their shipping charges, possibly due to rate hikes and packaging costs. This also makes their shipping more expensive than at other publishers.

KDP, while less costly to print, also takes 20% commission but on the list price, and gives you more back in the form of net revenues. For a 100 page book listed at $17.95, they take $3.66 (printing) plus $3.59 (20%), so your net revenue will be $10.70. You figure your Unit Cost this way:

$$\text{Base Price} = \text{Print Cost} \times 3$$
$$\$3.66 \times 3 = \$10.98 \sim \$10.99$$

This is what you can actually price the book for and cover your unit cost and the commission on sales. So if you still want to price your book at $17.95, you will end up with this:

$$\$3.66 + (20\% \text{ of } \$17.95) = \text{Unit Cost}$$
$$\$3.66 + \$3.59 = \$7.25$$
$$\$17.95 - \$7.25 = \$10.70$$

KDP will list the book on Amazon for you, but Amazon takes more; double the commission or **40%**. So the book sold on Amazon for $17.95 will cost you **$10.84**. You would still end up with more than with Lulu: **$7.11**.

Unless you have a resale permit they also may charge sales tax on the books shipped to you for resale, but you must remember to add it to the cost of books sold, and look into getting a resale certificate from your home state. You will then be responsible for payment of the sales tax, but most booksellers typically collect the tax from their customers. More about this in the *Accounting For Sales And Operations* section.

But be careful about *KDP*. Remember that I discussed distribution with them? Unless you want to sell only to Amazon, or prefer to allow *KDP* to be listed as your publisher, it is not good for establishing your own imprint and publisher name.

Lightning Source (LSI), on the other hand, does not charge a commission on the sale of the book. Their whole income comes from the cost of production; and while they are a little pricey to set up the book at first they pay out the net revenues from the remainder (45%) when the standard wholesale discount (55%) is met on the sale per unit. The set up charge per title is $49, plus an annual catalog fee of $12 per title. They also charge $25 per revision as needed.

But they are connected to *Ingram Content Group* so the benefit of listing with them far exceeds the initial costs. Lightning Source can and will handle all wholesale distribution and sales for you, saving you the time and money involved with printing and shipping to retailers.

Recently, Lightning Source has divided itself into two entities: Lightning Source and Ingram Spark. Ingram Spark is devoted to small press publishers and authors who have a small list of books to sell, and LSI is now focused on multibook publishers who have whole catalogs of books to sell. Ingram Spark charges $49 to publish a book and $25 to publish revisions, though I must say there is no advantage to global distribution for ebooks. In the case of ebooks, they charge 60 cents per page to convert the raw file to an ebook. Their calculations for the Unit Cost of a book are no different than LSI.

For example, the **unit cost** of a 100 page book printed by **LSI** ($2.52), plus a handling fee of $1.99 and shipping cost of $3.80 (media mail) on the book. Add these together and you end up with **$8.31**. So using the wholesale discount you would be pricing the book at:

Unit Cost / .45 = List Price
$8.31 / .45 = $18.46 ~ $18.95 or $18.99

Notice that this comes out to a lot more than the list price we used before. But remember that you must figure in your desired royalty ($3.00), so your List Price can be set like this:

$2.52 + 1.99 + 3.80 + 3.00 = $11.31 / .45 = $25.18 ~ $24.95 or $24.99

A better way to do this is as follows:

$2.52 + 1.99 + 3.80 + 3.00 = $11.31 x 2 = $22.62 ~ $22.95 or $22.99

Once you see the value of pricing a book this way, you can sell the books and not have to worry about what the cover price is to retailers. Your royalty may be slightly less per book sold, but the book will sell better at the lower price. So any real loss is negligable. The retailers buy the book at the printing cost level and mark up the price or discount it accordingly. Again, the SRP is in play. It is up to you to decide which price to use.

As you can see on the back cover of any book, the list price is often printed, and may be shown in multiple currencies allowing for exchange rates between countries, but even if it is not most of the major booksellers work on an honor system where they agree to hold to the price listed in **Books in Print**.

Depending on the wholesale discount, the retailer can then lower the sale price when it offers any discount as necessary. After all, they have to make a profit, too. You must take this into consideration when pricing your book.

If the book is taken out of circulation or retired, its collectible value will determine what price it will be sold at next. I have seen some outrageous prices charged for *used books* because of this, depending on their market or intrinsic value. Note that I am not talking about books which are in the public domain or have historical or antiquarian value.

Remember that I said you have no control over this. The marketplace is wild and untamable where pricing is concerned. Only the readers or buyers will determine at which price the book will actually sell. But if you do not want to deal with that sort of limitation, you can leave the price off the cover of your book, and this means that the marketplace will determine the price of the book based on the printing cost. Most booksellers will still honor the price set at the supplier's suggestion.

The Cost Averaging Method. Most publishers do not use this method because they have already decided which printer to use, but if you are selling your book across a range of different selling sources, you can also take the total of the production costs and divide it by the number of sources you are using to bring your price down. This is risky; at some point you may not find it useful.

Say you have the 100 page book printed through KDP, Lulu and LSI. You remember I said it costs $3.66 from KDP, $6.53 at Lulu, and $2.52 at LSI.

$$\$6.53 + \$3.66 + \$2.52 = \$12.71 \rightarrow \$12.71 / 3 = \$4.24$$

You can use this number to figure a retail price which is closer to the desired range for your book. When you add in your $3 royalty you will come up with this:

$$\text{Unit Cost} = \$4.24 + \$3.00 = \$7.24$$
$$\text{List Price} = \$7.24 / .45 = \$16.08 \sim \$16.95 \text{ or } \$16.99$$

This is how you can also determine how much leeway you have for costs between the three printing sources. Remember that no matter which way you price it, the book's sale will still yield your $3 of royalty. The averaging method should ideally be used when your books have been sitting for a while or sales have begun to decline at a higher price.

You then calculate your unit costs against the retail price *you* set (accounting for the sales commissions) to determine your royalty or net revenue:

$$\$16.95 - 7.13 = \$9.82 \text{ (Lulu)}$$
$$\$16.95 - 7.05 = \$9.90 \text{ (KDP)}$$
$$\$16.95 - 10.44 = \$6.51 \text{ (KDP/Amazon)}$$
$$\$16.95 - 11.84 = \$5.11 \text{ (LSI)}$$
(accounting for the wholesale discount)

You see that even if you calculate each store's take differently, you still come out slightly ahead on royalties with the *cost averaging method*.

Depending on which payment processor you use, the net revenues from sales on your own site will be even more. The cost of shipping comes into play again, so you should include the cost of shipping to yourself in the unit cost projection.

You can do this with all of your products across the range of your product line. If you succeed in reducing your list prices for them you will increase their saleable value. The costs to produce each product can be stated this way especially when you want to aggregate the costs for each product type. The difference in cost is increased when the lower of the various printing costs is used, but this way you have a cushion to work with.

Sometimes you have no choice but to increase your retail price to account from a net increase in your costs. In that case, you use the *highest* cost of printing to recalculate your unit cost. Always try to recover every cost you incur so that your income is not reduced.

Discounts and Their Uses

In addition to the wholesale discount on the list price, you must know when and how to use discounts on sales. You always have the option to lower the price permanently, but you can offer a discount when you want to sell your book faster during certain times of the year, or when you think your book was priced too high to begin with. Everyone in the book industry posts deep discounts on the sale of books during the last quarter of the calendar year to drive holiday sales. This is when they try to recoup the losses they incurred during the rest of the year or when the economy is bad.

If you are selling the book yourself, not only is your unit cost covered, so is your royalty; and since you are not charging yourself the wholesale discount all that extra money is there to work with. But this can also be a disadvantage if you want to sell the book at a retail discount.

If you think the list price is a little high, you can cut the price 25% to see if anyone will buy the book at the lower price. For instance if you kept the original price of your book at *$17.95*, **$17.95 x .75 = $13.46~ $13.95 or $13.99**. There is your new price. If this does not attract buyers you can cut the price another 10%. So you set it up as **$17.95 x .65 = $11.67 ~ $11.95 or $11.99**.

But just remember this. Your discounted or sale price must never go below your unit cost for the book or you will be losing money on the whole deal. Using the *cost averaging method,* here is how your book royalty looks at this point:

$$\$11.67 - \$8.31 = \$3.36$$

This is your **profit margin** per book. You notice that the profit margin falls dangerously close to your royalty and excludes other overhead costs to sell the book, as well as the monthly costs for your operations outside of printing and selling.

Try to set a discount which satisfies both requirements, which can be calculated this way:

Price - Unit Cost = Discount
$$\$17.95 - \$8.31 = \$9.64 \rightarrow \$9.64 - \$7.24 = \$2.64$$

This tells you that you can set your price as much as $2.64 below your regular price for a discount which does not take your sale below the unit cost for the book and still allow for your $3.00 royalty. If you are selling the books it is the *net revenues* which will govern your discount calculations, not the retail price. There is also the danger that you might set the price of the book too low for the actual market value, so you would be undercutting yourself.

In fact, if you find that you want to charge an integer amount for a price, you can. So if you charge $18.00 for a book, your royalty will be expressed as more or less depending on your wholesale discount.

We have not taken into account the **rate of returns** on the sales of the book. It is a fact that some books will be returned based on who you are dealing with, the consumer or the bookseller, and only if your service allows for returns.

Say you sell 100 books in a given month and 10 books are returned. Your *unit cost per book* will then increase by the amount you estimate: 10% of list price, or $1.80. You must make an adjustment to the unit cost, thus:

Unit Cost = $7.24 + $1.80 = $9.04
$$\$17.95 - \$9.04 = \$8.91 \rightarrow \$8.91 - \$7.24 = \$1.67$$

This reduces the amount of the retail discount you can work with and still cover your unit costs over a given sales period. Your own unit cost for each book sold may vary depending on the number and type of costs you add in, the trim size and format, and so on; but this calculation must be performed to give you a good picture of how much you have to work with.

You also have to account for the discount when you are recording your sales. In this way you can hedge the loss on sales and maintain a good estimate of the *saleable value* of the book. By saleable value, I mean the price at which your book will continue to sell over time.

If after a year your sales may begin to drop off for a particular title, or if you are not satisfied with the price you set, you can lower it to drive sales. You can do this by lowering your royalty to lower your unit cost or by switching to a different publisher, or even using a different shipping method. Remember that *you* are in control of all aspects of publishing your book even if you cannot negotiate with your printer for a better deal on printing. But you must be prepared to take a cut in gross income in order to drive sales.

Costs of production are considered to be *fixed* costs; that is, they are usually the same over a long period of time until they are adjusted for increases, inflation, or adjustments made to account for changes in your overall selling program.

Calculate Your Costs of Sales

As I mentioned before, your book sales will be reduced by certain costs which are not part of the costs of production. And I also discussed how discounts are used to make the book attractive at the price you set.

Costs of sales, aside from the commissions collected by your publishing service, include the following:

Sales tax
Shipping and Handling
Packaging and Displays
Promotional giveaways
Samples
Employee commissions and/or wages
Storefront or web site costs
Credit card processing charges
Promotions and advertising

In general, the way to distribute these costs across the whole selling operation is to total your sales costs and divide them by the total number of books sold in a given period. Costs of sales are said to be *variable* costs; that is, they are costs which will change constantly from period to period.

Total Costs of Sales (COS) / Number of Books Sold =
Unit Costs of Sales

You then take this unit cost and add it to the Unit Cost of Production (COP). For a little shorthand, I will show it to you this way:

COP + COS = Unit Cost
List Price – Unit Cost = Net Operating Margin

In the next section I will help you understand this in a little more depth.

Accounting For Sales And Operations

Get out your pencil or calculator and roll up your sleeves, because here is where the magic of creating the records you need to keep an accurate account of your business begins. As a publishing author, your knowledge of how your business works is just as important to your success as your ability to write and publish a book. If you have never done any of this before, the details can be both daunting and confusing, but do not panic. Once you learn how to keep your own books you will have more time to write.

Types of Business Entities

If you have never managed or started a business before, you have a wide range of options open to you. When you are just starting out as a book seller, whether online or in person, there are several types of businesses you can establish with just a little money.

The **Sole Proprietorship** (DBA) - the moment you declare you are in business, you are a business. Everything you do places you at risk for your business. Even if you have employees to help you, the business is yours. Depending on the type of business you do you are personally liable for business taxes if you operate a store or outside office, various types of licenses, insurance, and other taxes as relate to your business. If you are operating only as a mail order firm or online, your base is in your home and you may be able to deduct the expenses of your home as part of your business on your federal income tax return. If you travel extensively, your travel expenses may also be counted.

The **Limited Liability Company** (LLC) - usually a small or specialty business which is managed by a service organization. Some law firms and specialty security and insurance companies are often formed this way.

The **Limited Partnership** (Ltd.) - a pair or group of individuals form a business and divide the risks and costs of operations, as well as the profits, among them. They may not be divided equally. Often the Ltd. Partnership is owned by a majority partner or founder and/or senior partners, with associate partners sharing in the rest of the division. The partnership is formed by agreement among all concerned, and is dissolved by mutual agreement. New partners may be accepted to the existing partnership only by unaminous consent.

The **Small Business Corporation** (SBC) - You can incorporate yourself and name your small business as an SBC to defer your financial risk to the assets and the expenses of the business alone. This protects your personal assets, like your home and automobile, from liability or litigation; and makes the business itself liable for any tax liens or damages arising from its operation. It also makes you the sole owner and chief financial officer of your business.

But it is only useful if your success results in a large amount of money changing hands on a daily basis. If you are an individual bookseller, it may not be necessary to incorporate. Your risk is only limited to sales, costs of operations, and your business tax liability.

The **Corporation** (Inc.) - this kind of business exists where a product requires more structure and cash flow than a bookseller will ever need starting out. For example, Amazon.com is a corporation, as is Barnes & Noble, Borders, Lulu, KDP, and so on. The corporation is managed by the owners, who are a cadre of individuals responsible for its operations, shareholders if the corporation is "publicly owned", and a board of officers responsible for its management.

But if you are interested in starting out on a shoestring budget, getting incorporated this way involves a great deal more money and financial risk than you may be able to handle.

To learn more about these kinds of businesses and what may be best for your particular circumstances, I suggest you visit *www.nolo.com*, a public service site which provides law information and forms for creating your own business. Some of their services may be pricey, but you can also call or visit your local city and state government offices to get the forms for free, and for information on what is necessary to get started in your area.

Basic Bookkeeping For The Beginner

If you have no idea how to keep a record of your income and expenses here is where to start. Even if you have a fair knowledge of bookkeeping, please read through to refresh your education. If you can afford a bookkeeping program like *QuickBooks* by all means use one, but you still have to learn the basic concepts in order to understand the hard numbers.

The **business year** is only 360 days long for bookkeeping purposes. You can continue to conduct business 365 days a year, but that means you chose to do business on the five major holidays: New Year's Day, Memorial Day, July 4th, Thanksgiving and Christmas Day. The accounting cycle can be shortened or lengthened depending on when you choose to do business. Some businesses are open 6 to 9 months of the year; others year round, 24 hours a day. Many which operate on the typical 12 month calendar year shorten it by five days in December in order to pass earnings and expenses incurred during that time to the next operating year. After all, no one wants to be sitting there cooking the books on New Year's Day. When you conduct business on a holiday you still account for it on the next *business* day's record.

Other businesses start on the day of their official formation, called a fiscal year. For example, the fiscal year of the state of California begins on July 1. Many businesses which perform services for the state also begin their fiscal years on that day. But for federal tax purposes you are better off starting it on January 1, otherwise, you will have account for a *timing difference* in your business activities.

The basic goal of your operations is to make money, but you must account for that activity based on this rule:

$$\text{Assets} = \text{Liabilities} + \text{Capital}$$
$$\text{or}$$
$$\text{Assets} - \text{Liabilities} = \text{Capital}$$

Capital refers to the retained earnings of your business after your liabilities have been met. **Assets** are anything you own, tangible and intangible (like intellectual property and copyrights), which have a monetary value. The equation must always be in balance. So a reduction in your **liabilities** equals an increase in capital. This equation is an expression of the net worth of your business. When your assets far exceed your liabilities, then your business is healthy. When your liabilities far exceed your assets, you are bankrupt.

Two *accounting methods* are used to account for your **operating income** are the *cash* method and the *accrual* method.

Cash method: you record and account for all cash received and all costs and expenses paid *within* the fiscal or calendar year. If you are owed money but have not been paid yet, the rule is that you wait until you are paid to record the amount received. You move the recorded sale to the next year if the payment has not been received as of December 25 or the end of your fiscal year*. If you owe money you record the payment on the payment date, not the date when it becomes due. In this way you can defer unearned income and unpaid expenses to the next year. This has certain tax advantages which include the above, but also can reduce your tax liability over a year in which you may incur a loss if your costs were higher than anticipated or planned for. *This is not a hard rule. You can keep recording income until midnight Dec. 31 if you want to.

Accrual method: you record and account for all income and expenses whether they were paid or not. You maintain two accounts for the money you are owed (*accounts receivable*) and the money you owe (*accounts payable*), to offset against your actual income and expenses over the year. This method has tax disadvantages but is a more accurate picture of your net worth over the year. If you work with printers which invoice you for services performed instead of up front, the accrual method will cover this aspect of your business very well, but if you are just starting out the *cash* method is best.

Then, if you find you are running a prosperous business after all you can switch accounting methods, but you must tell the IRS about the switch or there may be problems down the road.

Journals You keep a running record of each account you use in your business operations in a series of *journals* to segregate the money according to its purpose and importance. If you are working out of your checkbook, you know the basic *double entry* system employed in bookkeeping already.

Journals enable you to record various transactions and help you track where the money goes in your operations. Certain accounts also have a specific place on your balance sheet, so their treatment in each journal will have a certain weight. They are looked at as *debits (dr)* and *credits (cr)*, just like in your checkbook, only their treatment is the exact opposite of your checkbook, which operates on the premise that

Balance = Credits – Debits.

The bank sees every deposit you make to your account as money they owe you, just as every check or withdrawal of cash you make is a reduction in their liability. However, in your case the opposite applies.

Sales Journal. All transactions as they relate to sales are recorded here.

Cash Receipts Journal. All transactions where cash is received are recorded here, including cash from sales and cash received from credit sales, payments on *accounts receivable*, and so on. Cash receipts add to your net income. Special columns where you are likely to add or subtract cash are also included in this journal.

You can add as many columns as you need to make this journal useful to you. This relates only to *cash you received* and nothing else.

Purchases Journal. Here is where you record your purchases for whatever purpose. It includes cash and credit purchases of assets which are going to be written off over time or taken against your sales activity.

Cash Payments Journal. Here is where you record all your cash outlays for whatever purpose. It is different from the cash receipts journal in that you must also account for all the different kinds of assets and services you are paying for. Here I show only three asset accounts, but you can include as many columns as are necessary to complete your journal.

Special Journals. The two which apply specifically to your book business are the *Purchases Returns and Allowances Journal* and the *Sales Returns and Allowances Journal*. These are used to track the pattern of purchases and sales which give an indication of the condition of your inventories. In this way you can mitigate some of the problems you are likely to encounter.

If you find that you are having to return books you ordered due to defects in production or shipping damages on a regular basis, the **Purchases Returns and Allowances Journal** allows you to detect a pattern of problems with your printer or publisher.

You can use this data to confront your supplier and ask about the specific shipments involved, or try to change the shipping method. It is best when you can come up with cold hard numbers so that there is no ambiguity or confusion when you speak to your supplier. You use the invoice number to help track the specific shipment, or if you have a shipment number you can track that on an extra column.

You can also insert a column to track the problem with a specific book or title. Are there two versions of the same book? Is there another author using the same title printing through Acme? Was there an error in the input of the order? Was the order not fulfilled? and so on.

The **Sales Returns and Allowances Journal**. Sometime it is just a matter of selling less defective goods. But this journal also helps you to track the buying habits of specific or regular customers over the year.

In the retail world there are certain people who buy things, use them once and then try to return them later for a full refund. Some of these people also try to return them without a receipt to back up the purchase. There are still others who will buy your product at a different retailer and then try to sell it back to you without a receipt, or think that the receipt from the other retailer ought to be enough to get their money. These are called *grifters*. They are concerned with nothing but getting the full advantage of an item's use for nothing, or with getting the money itself.

But you have a legal recourse: if you find that a particular customer keeps returning items to you, you can ask why and/or refuse to sell to that customer.

This record will protect you in any court of law, and you can back it up with a sample of the evidence along with the physical copy of the invoice and shipping order.

If you are reasonably tech savvy you can keep a series of spreadsheets with links to others for each journal, in one workbook so you don't lose the data and can have it close at hand. The old pencil journals are long gone, and if you are not proficient at bookkeeping you should invest in a bookkeeping program or service to make your life easier.

Ledgers - Each account has its own ledger for making additions and subtractions as well as adjustments. They are also known as "T" accounts because you are keeping the balance in the accounts equal. For example, you track cash as one account in one ledger, accounts receivables in another, inventory in another, and so on. In this way you can verify the accuracy of your numbers by seeing them together on one report.

If they are not balanced at the end of the period, you make an adjusting entry to bring them into balance. But do not fall into the habit of making an adjustment instead of checking your entries. If you find that you cannot balance your accounts you need to double check your records to see if there is something missing or unaccounted for. The devil is in the details.

Calculate Your Income and Expenses

When you are conducting your business you have to calculate certain formulas in order to see the results of your hard work. Here is a basic picture of the whole enchilada:

Operating Income = Net Revenues - Operating Expenses

How you record your sales and your unit costs determines your net revenues. Your operating expenses include asset offset expenses like depreciation, amortization, and good will (more about this later).

The Sales Summary is your *net revenues* as they relate directly to the income and expenses associated with the sales of your book. It represents the total of book sales across the whole range of the booksellers and customers you work with. Say you only have two publishers who sell your books for you. You can use Microsoft Excel or an Apple Mac software spreadsheet to see a clear picture of your sales at any time.

In order to prepare the summary you have to do some detail work to arrive at the numbers. You can get as specific as you want at this point. You can break up the sales from each seller, including yourself, into separate sheets. The catalog number may depend on each seller. For LSI and Amazon, for example, the catalog number per book is the 10 digit version of the ISBN.

For Barnes & Noble is it always the 13 digit number. If you are more savvy about this you can keep a log by catalog number alone and leave off the book's title, but for a more complete report you should add the title in a separate column. You can also do this for yourself if you plan to sell books in person at a specific venue like a book fair.

Sales Detail Report - the report which presents the true picture of your sales and expenses. This includes the title, the catalog number, your vendor's catalog number, the sales price, discounts, total sales, and all the costs associated with printing and delivery of your book. It also includes the terms of payment to you the supplier. This will become important to your choice of recording method.

You can still use the *cash method* by recording only the amount you receive each reporting period, but be sure to carry over the unpaid sales which overlap into your next fiscal or calendar year. **net/30** means you receive the net revenues less the *costs of production* within 30-90 days **after** the end of the month in which the books were sold. If you have 9 books, you add a row for each book in your catalog that you have placed with them. At the end of the year, you total all the amounts earned on each book for inclusion in your **sales summary**. Most sellers use the net/60 method, however, so you will have to wait longer for the money.

You take the *wholesale discount* only when the books are sold through a distributor, or a selling printer like *LSI*. It reduces your net revenues from sales. Returns are recorded when you must accept them, otherwise they are accounted for when your seller reports your sales.

The *discount on sales* is recorded as a *percentage* of the gross amount based on the list price of the book and is taken only when you set it. This is important for sales and sales tax purposes. Usually you can look up the figures in your service's monthly compensation report, which shows how many books sold, the printing cost and the net compensation from the transaction.

The **sales detail report** can be filled in on a monthly, quarterly, or semiannual basis, depending on the volume of your sales activity. If you think you will sell books consistently across the whole year, you can also prepare a detail summary for addition to the master summary. Just remember to figure in your actual unit costs at the end.

The Profit Margin

Now, here is where you get a clear picture of what you have left to work with to cover your operating costs.

Profit Margin = Net Revenues - Unit Costs

Remember that I said you can add in all the costs associated with the production and sales of your book, so to determine this you can put up a spreadsheet that segregates the costs into their individual elements. This is especially helpful when you want to see how much each book costs to create and sell. Note that the shipping cost attached to the sale of a book you sold can be recorded here, as well as whatever sales tax you collected.

As an alternative you could extend your **Sales Detail Report** to record your **profit margin** in one fell swoop by combining both reports on the same page. You may have to print it out in landscape orientation to see the whole picture, but your spreadsheet for sales can then be as detailed as you want.

The *profit margin* is the amount you have left to use to offset other expenses of running your business, such as office expenses and utilities, business taxes, and other costs. If you do not make enough from the sales of your book to cover these, you realize a negative income. But do not worry about that right now.

Operating Income and Expenses

The expenses you incur and pay over the course of your operating year are of a specific kind. You keep a record of these in the receipts you collect whenever you pay for them, and also in the record of their occurrence. These are expenses you pay to run your business and meet your tax obligations to the city, county, state and nation.

Operating Income = Profit Margin - Operating Expenses

Here is a list of the common expenses you will record over the year:

Sales Tax Expense - If you owe the sales tax on any sale of your book from the previous year, you record the expense here. You accrue the sales tax whenever you sell a book yourself in the state where you reside. You pay this tax to your state's excise tax board after the end of the year. *The report is NOT for income tax; only for sales tax.* The way to offset this obligation is to collect it at the time of sale and then include it in your gross sales amount. In this case, no matter what method of accounting you use, you still record the tax as a *liability* as part of your net worth, by means of the account *Sales Taxes Payable.*

Sales Tax Payable = Gross Sales x Sales Tax % per location
Sales Tax Expense = Sales Tax Payable - current year's tax

There will always be a residual amount of the tax carried over into the next year because of rounding. For example: in California's sales tax computation, all amounts are rounded up or down to the nearest dollar depending on the total of the tax owed. This will always leave out a few pennies from the payment. Over time, this amount can accrue to more than a dollar. At times you might find that you have collected the sales tax for sales in a county which has dropped the local tax, in which case you may have to hold that money indefinitely.

But here is a way to get rid of it. When you take the expense, you include the *residual* amount for the previous year on your sales tax report. This empties out the payable column and makes it ready for the current year's collection. You never transfer the residual tax into another expense account or your gross income. This is considered *illegal*. To avoid that you could **charge only the *state* portion of the tax on sales and then remit the county and local taxes as an expense in the next year**. In that case, you will still end up with a zero amount in your payable column. If by chance your state raises the base tax, you then have a small amount of time to determine if the amount you kept will cover the difference. The way to avoid surprises like this is to monitor your state's tax legislation through the web site they maintain. Changes in the sales tax could also go in your favor.

When you perform the calculation for net revenues the amount will include the sales tax collected. You can then extract the sales tax and record it in *sales tax payable.*

An alternate solution is to add a sales tax estimate to your *list price*. But remember that you want to drive sales, not appease the tax man. Raising the price will not increase your earning potential and lowers the saleable value of your book.

You do not have this obligation when a seller collects and pays it for you. For internet sales you can leave this tax out of the equation, but be prepared for an audit by the state you reside in. More and more states are trying to make it possible to collect on online sales depending on where you make your base of operations in order to pad their own revenues; but right now they are focused on the big sellers like *Amazon* and are not too concerned with small businesses.

Beginning on September 15 of 2012, Amazon was forced to start collecting sales tax from Californian customers as part as a settlement deal with the state. Since then, the number of states which it must collect tax for has risen to 32. However, the issue of legislating a national sales tax has made many online sellers protest. Collecting the sales tax from the consumer has always been a deal killer.

To avoid the headache of dealing with the tax man I make a habit of pricing everything I sell with the sales tax included as a part of my *costs of sales*, which means that even if I do not collect the tax from the customer, I can still remit the tax to my state at the end of the year. This remittance is confined only to the sales I make within my state.

Generally, you can deduct the amount of tax for out of state deliveries from the amount you owe depending on the state you live in. If your state does not collect the tax at all you have nothing to worry about.

Much of the difficulty states have with gaining tax revenues stems from the fact that even though shoppers owe use tax on items they purchased, they never report or pay the tax. So the burden is placed on the sellers to collect it, and they are now seen by shoppers as evil money grubbers; quite wrongly, I may add. If the shoppers knew how close they are to being audited by the state they would not be grumbling, but there it is. The best thing to do is grin and bear it.

Bad debt expense - This expense is taken when you have exhausted all efforts to collect on a debt, especially when you sell books on credit or by the accrual method of accounting. Normally, you segregate your sales into two components:

Gross Sales = Cash Received + Accounts Receivable

The bad debt expense is taken from your *Accounts Receivable* account and is a write off expense. You established this account because you expect to be paid at a future date. You take the expense once a year to account for the loss for tax purposes, and also to give the creditor time to pay the amount owed over the year.

You determine the expense by *ageing* receivables in your account; that is, making sure that the receivables are old enough to be written off by looking at when the receivables were first recorded.

If you employ the *cash method*, however, your gross sales are only recorded when you are paid. But if you delivered the product to your customer before payment, you must keep track of it so I would advise setting up accrual accounts for the unpaid balances anyway.

Say you have already been paid for most of the amounts owed to you, but there are a few holdouts:

Accounts Receivable - Cash Received = Allowance for Bad Debts

This is a "contra-asset" account and contains the amounts outstanding. In this way you can refresh the original account with new receivables. If you have only a few creditors to begin with and they still refuse to pay, you simply take the exact amount in dispute and expense it as a *Bad Debt Expense*.

If by chance a debtor you have written off pays you later, you write it as *cash received* in the year it was paid. Your *Bad Debt Expense* account should remain empty.

To record the back payment: **Cash Received = Other Income**

If you have a large number of people who owe you money and have not paid, you can take a percentage of the total receivables and write it off whether you are paid later or not.

Bad Debt Expense = Accounts Receivable x Estimated %

Then you also need to ask yourself why you are relying heavily on credit to get paid in the first place if you find you are saddled with so many deadbeats. To reduce the need to use this expense often you might have to switch to a *prepaid payment* schedule instead of payment from invoices and deliveries. You might anger some of the customers but they will be the ones who are stiffing you in the first place. The rest will understand and continue to buy from you.

Domain name and web site hosting fees like email boxes and FTP (web hosting) space, payment processing, shareware fees and so on. You record these when you pay them.

Travel expenses. If you embark on a book signing tour most of this will come out of your own pocket. Traditional publishers are no longer shelling out for travel expenses without a significant contribution from their authors. If you have published your own books you are on your own. These expenses include: *hotel room, meals,* and *transportation,* which includes gas and mileage for your car. Note that tips and gratuities are no longer counted. The watchword is that if you can avoid these extra expenses you are two steps ahead of the game.

There are also certain *distance limitations* to this expense. For example, you cannot take the expense if the book signing is held in your own community or within fifty miles of your base of operations. For this reason it is vitally important that you keep your receipts and write on them what they are for, and what event they relate to. Personal items such as toothbrushes, other toiletries and clothing, however, are not covered.

Advertising and promotion. This includes the costs of print ads, business cards, promotional materials and giveaways for your book and your publishing company, the cost of review copies and press kits. It also includes fees paid to professional marketers and promoters working on your behalf.

Postage and Shipping. This includes the amount paid for shipping your books to your customers, direct mailing, regular correspondence and the supplies consumed in the process; like boxes, envelopes, padded envelopes and tubes, bubblewrap, foam and stryrofoam popcorn. The reason you take it here is that it is a *disposable* expense. You expect to use these items only once, though I have received items back in the mail and recycled the packaging materials instead of using new.

Selling supplies, including plastic and paper bags, receipt and order pads, credit card slips, and other *disposable* promotional supplies like free pens, candies and so on. You track these separately from office supplies because they are more disposable and difficult to track. You expense the whole amount at the end of the year even if you have some left over. Some companies choose to keep a Petty Cash account just to cover these ephemeral expenses.

Office supplies. Pencils and pens, staples, staplers, boxcutter blades, notepads, printer ink, paper towels, stationery and other *disposable* supplies. You determine the expense by itemizing your purchases over the year through receipts, then taking a percentage of the total. Some people write off the whole amount at the end of the year.

Rentals. Many small businesses use this expense to offset their income, so there is no reason why you cannot do the same.

If you work out of your home, you may be able to take a portion of your mortgage payments as a *home office expense* for tax purposes. If you rent or lease space for an outside office or bookstore you take the total of your payments for the year. If you work out of your apartment, you can take the portion of your rent which relates to the amount of space you use for your work.

Rental expenses also include the costs of booth or display space if you sell at book fairs, art festivals, conventions and other venues where you reserve allotted space to display your goods.

The expense includes the rental of furniture such as canopies, tables, chairs and display racks. If you own these items already you can take a depreciation expense at the end of the year to offset their cost.

Salaries Expense. If you are a small press publisher with employees, here is where you record the salaries you paid out for the year. Salaries are taxable, and are recorded in an account called ***Salaries Payable***. The salaries earned are held until paid out, net of withholdings for each pay period. Salaries are often stated as a fixed cost because they tend to be the same amount every pay period.

Bonuses are even less frequent and should be kept in their own account, called ***Bonuses Payable***.

Wages Payable is recorded for hourly employees. Wages include overtime, sick pay and other more variable amounts which change from month to month.

These names may seem boring but they are necessary to give you a picture of the amount of *liabilities* you are likely to incur in a given pay period. They are add to the amount of accrued deductions you take to pay your state, local, and federal agencies.

Payroll Tax Expense - This includes Social Security, state disability insurance, unemployment insurance and other employee taxes paid during the year. This is the aggregate amount collected among the individual accounts and kept in one account called *Payroll Taxes Payable*. The expense is reported and paid to the individual taxing entities, usually on a quarterly basis. You keep a record of each on a spreadsheet for that purpose.

Net Pay is the amount of payroll you pay out to your employees. You record the totals of the payables into their individual accounts. Here is where the magic of accounting for your income and expenses occurs.

In the *cash* method you take the expense of each according to what you paid during the year. For example, if you pay twice a month and have not paid the amounts aggregated as of 12/15, you subtract them from your expenses and leave the remainder in the payable accounts. They should be paid out on December 31.

In the *accrual* method you take the whole amount as an expense whether you paid it or not. This can lead to some disadvantages when it comes to income tax reporting so to be safe you should always account in the cash method even if you have payables to deal with.

Either way you should keep individual amounts of taxes and other obligations separate for your peace of mind. Your payables can also be grouped according to their relevence or type.

Insurance Expense - Of course, if you do not have an insurance policy on losses incurred during the course of your business, such as damages to your business property, theft, vandalism, and fire, you can leave this off your net income statement. But if you do, you can take the premium payments as an expense. You also take the payouts to you as *unearned income*, which you can then use to pay for repairs and replacements immediately.

Utilities Expense - Electricity, gas, cell phone or walkie time, and other energy expenses that directly relate to your business. If you work mostly with your cell phone this is especially helpful. But be careful. If you work out of your home you can only take the same percentage as you took for your home rent expense.

Charitable contributions - These are expenses associated with your sponsorship of or a contribution to a charity which directly relates to your business. This can include education, television station contributions and sports. But be careful not to devote too much money to this as you are limited to take half whatever you paid out for tax purposes. Some of these charities are also excluded from the list of those allowable by the IRS.

Repairs - Sooner or later something will break. This is not the same as additions, improvements or upgrades, which I will discuss later.

Interest Expense - This is the interest you pay on your *business* loans and lines of credit. Personal credit card interest does not count. Say you got a $25,000 infusion of cash for operations from your local bank. You take the interest you paid on the principal of the loan during the year.

Depreciation and Amortisation Expenses - These are discussed in the *Asset Expenses* section.

Miscellaneous Expenses - Depending on your activity, you can also take expenses which relate directly to your profession and your business. If you buy a magazine which you need to finish a book, you can record the purchase here. Magazines are considered *disposable.* You can also record the membership fee for your local author's association, and other items which do not fit under the above classifications *which are expected to expire within the year*. Convention memberships and the like may also be included.

But be careful. This number can become wildly inflated and the IRS frowns on the overuse of this expense. If you have recorded small amounts elsewhere and your miscellaneous expenses are the only big number on your balance sheet, the IRS may audit you.

Asset Expenses

Now that you have been acquainted with the operating expenses, I am going to reintroduce you to the concept you learned before:

Capital = Assets – Liabilities

This is the basic picture of your financial condition. The three elements are always in balance. You could call it the *feng shui* of your business.

Assets are all the items which you use in your business and which make up your net worth. Your assets include: cash, accounts receivables, inventories, office supplies, selling supplies, office equipment, display equipment, copyrights and other intellectual properties, insurance, prepaid rent, long term leases, and other assets which relate directly to your business.

Liabilities are all the payables and debts you owe in order to conduct your business. For example, payroll tax payable, sales taxes payables, accounts payable owed on services and printing, and so on. These reduce the value of your business net worth.

Capital represents the effect of the increase or decrease of your business value over the year, and includes net income.

Beginning Capital = Assets – Liabilities

Net Income = Operating Income - Operating Expenses

Ending Capital =
(Assets - Liabilities) + (Net Income - Drawing) + Misc Income

Asset Expenses are the expenses you take to write off the purchases of long-term assets you own over the year. There are two types; *depreciation* and **amortisation**. *Why do I need to do this?* you ask. Because you want to recover the costs of these assets and reduce your taxable income for income tax purposes. Remember that any expense which does this is a benefit to you.

Copyrights, trademarks and other intellectual properties are called *intangible assets*; that is, assets which are not physical but which have a monetary value nonetheless. Copyrights and publication rights also retain their value through the life of the book and its author, and up to 70 years beyond the author's death.

Copyrights and intellectual property are *not* depreciated or amortised because they remain constantly in use over your life, not the life of the business. But their monetary value is listed as part of your business assets because they are an integral part of your operations. If you cannot make a reasonable estimate of their value over the life of your businss you can leave them off. You can also leave them off if you think their intrisic value will overinflate the true taxable value of your business.

Generally, you should at least count the cost to register your copyrights and trademark as the value of your intangible assets.

Depreciation is the write off of costs associated with the purchase and disposal of long-term *physical* assets. These include: office furniture, computers, office equipment, plant and printing equipment, display equipment and furniture, books and research materials used for your business.

You write off the purchase or decrease in value of an item by means of a depreciation or contra-asset account called *Accumulated Depreciation*. You keep a separate account for each asset to be depreciated, and add the expense to the Accumulation account over the life of the asset. You retain these values on your books over the life of your business until you retire, dispose of or sell off the asset.

There are two ways you can calculate the amount of depreciation over the course of an asset's useful life. Say you bought a computer for use in your business. You add it to your list of assets as *Computers*. You set up a depreciation account called *Accumulated Depreciation - Computers*.

Since a computer is expected to last no more than about five years on average, you can use **accelerated depreciation** to determine the depreciation expense. You divide the purchase amount (the total including sales tax and shipping) by 5 (20%). You then divide the 20% by 360. You expense the depreciation each month by taking the unit amount per day and multiplying it by the number of days in the month. *This means that in a 28 day month you multiply it by 28*. Then you add the expense to the contra-asset account.

Depreciation Expense = [(Computer Cost / 5) / 360] x Days

Accumulated Depreciation = Depreciation Expense1

But you are not finished. As you compute this expense over the expected life of your asset, the amount you expense each month is reduced by the *remainder* of the balance of the two accounts.

Asset - Accumulated Depreciation = Residual Value
Depreciation Expense2 = [(Residual Value / 5) / 360] x Days
Accumulated Depreciation = Depr Exp1 + Depr Exp2

and so on.

If you have a desktop computer which you expect to use for ten years, this accelerated depreciation helps you to write off the purchase faster. I did not include the printer or other peripheral equipment here but you can lump them all together into the same account if they were purchased at the same time and from the same place.

Either way you do it, the depreciation expense is taken as shown above. You account for the depreciation of each item separately depending on when it was bought.

When you have long term physical assets like plant and *printing equipment*, however, you take a different approach. You depreciate these over a longer period, like ten years. You can also account for their *salvage value*, an estimate of what they will sell for at the end of their useful lives. When you conduct your operations over the year you are normally expected to do this month to month.

Depr Exp1 = [([Equipment - Salvage] / 10) / 360] x Days
Accumulated Depreciation = Depr Exp1

Depr Exp2 = [([Residual Value - Salvage] / 10) / 360] x Days
Accumulated Depreciation = Depr Exp1 + Depr Exp2
and so on.

The *salvage value* of the asset is retained no matter how many years you expect to depreciate it. Remember that as the value of your asset declines, the amount of depreciation you can take in each month also declines. The amount will also increase or decrease if you purchase or dispose of similar assets during the course of the year. You must perform this calulation every month or year depending on how often you update your records.

If you clear your books once a year your expenses may be a little easier to work with. In that case:

Depr Expense = (Asset Cost - Salvage Value) / Year 1
Depr Expense2 = (Remainder - Salvage Value) / Year2
and so on.

The standard rule is that you account for each separate asset to get an accurate amount to be taken as an expense during the month. This can get quite complicated. You can keep a separate journal just for depreciation expenses by setting up a record of the purchase amounts and the dates you bought the assets, the number of years you decide to use for the expense of each, and so on.

If you do not have time to do all this, you can simplify this process by grouping your assets by time, such as assets to be depreciated in ten years, or five years, or any period you choose, and establishing an allowance account just for that group.

Group Depreciation Expense =
([(Group Total – Sum of Salvage Values) / years] / 360) x Days

In this way your group total will include new purchases and disposals over the year for assets in that group. The total amount of the expense will reflect the adjustments you made and eliminates the need to itemize to excess. You combine the expenses calculated for each group into the aggregate total of each asset type you want to depreciate:

Depreciation Expense =
5yr Group Depr Expense + 10 yr Group Depr Expense

Be sure that you create a report which summarizes the details for your financial statements when you fill out your 1040 Schedule C. This way you can keep track of how you arrived at the final expense numbers.

Amortisation - This is used to write off the costs associated with *intangible* assets like good will, leasehold improvements, start up costs and contracts. The *maximum* period to amortise these accounts is five years. You take the expense based on the same model used for accelerated depreciation.

$$\text{Amort Expense1} = [\,(\text{Asset Value}/5\,)/360\,] \times \text{Days}$$
$$\text{Accumulated Amortisation} = \text{Amortisation Exp1}$$

$$\text{Amort Expense2} = [\,(\text{Residual Value}/5\,)/360\,] \times \text{Days}$$
$$\text{Accumulated Amortisation} = \text{Amort Exp1} + \text{Amort Exp2}$$

Amortisation and depreciation are reported separately on your net income statement. You should never mix the type of assets you are expensing.

Inventory Control

When you are publishing books yourself, you have to decide which way you want your books to get to your customer. Inventory is considered a short-term asset because there is the *expectation* that you will sell it within the year.

Inventory does **not** include the costs of books which were printed and sold for you by your printer or online retailer. It only includes the books you keep on hand to sell. You can verify this amount by taking a physical count of the books in your garage at any time. You should have set up a spreadsheet to account for the sales of each *title* you own.

Suppose you want to keep a *physical* inventory of books at home and also work with POD printers.

Beginning inventory Jan 1
+ Purchases (books received from printer, including shipping*)
- Returns/Allowances (books returned to printer*)
- Current Inventory For Sale
= Costs of Goods Sold Dec. 31

*The shipping cost is usually borne by you the buyer as "FOB shipping point", unless your purchase terms include "FOB destination". It is kept separate from the regular shipping expense you incur during the course of your selling activity because it is added to your cost of the merchandise.

This presumes that you took an inventory at the end of the year. You can eliminate this time-consuming labor by recording your purchases, sales and adjustments over the course of the year through a *virtual inventory* spreadsheet and taking the total amounts left to arrive at the ending inventory.

The *ending inventory* also accounts for books resold, distributed to others or destroyed by you over the course of the year. The costs of books you sold directly to a customer are included in the total of *Costs of Goods Sold* for your Income Statement.

Sometimes you need to know the effects of your costs as they relate to your retail price. You took the total of ending inventory in order to compute your Cost of Goods Sold according to the actual costs. Here is another way of looking at it, called the **Retail Method** for costing inventory:

**Total Cost / Total Selling Price =
Ratio of Cost of Goods Sold to Net Sales**

For example, say you have 200 copies of a book which cost you $10 to produce and you are selling it at $18.95, but you have a net sales of $1,525 for 100 books. Using this equation, your ending merchandise inventory will be 52.7% of your net sales, or $803.68 ~ $804. If you compare it with your actual remainder of inventory ($1,000) you may find it a more cost effective way to arrive at Costs of Goods Sold because you will increase your Costs of Goods Sold to offset the discounts you took on the sales of the book.

$10 / $18.95 = .527 → .527 x $1525 = $804

Beginning Inventory Jan 1	$1,000
+ Purchases	1,000
- Returns and Allowances	0
- Ending Inventory Dec 31	804
Cost of Goods Sold Dec. 31	$1,196

When you do this, your *Operating Income* decreases by the difference between the total of sales and the total costs, including the amount of discounts and returns you incurred during the sales period. But be careful, as you will still have to account for that reduction in the value of your inventory somewhere in your records at the beginning of the next year.

Profit Margin = Net Sales - Costs of Goods Sold

This is the part that becomes important for you to arrive at your Net Income and Balance Sheets, which will be discussed in the next section.

Financial Statements

Depending on whatever accounting method you use, you want to arrive at a clear picture of what your business activity looks like at the end of the year for tax purposes. The IRS Schedule C is what you use to report your business income and expenses. But in order to fill in the right numbers you will have to organize your information into various forms.

The Operating Income Statement This is the statement of your net profit or loss during the year and is the main part of the report. You notice that the Operating Income accounts for the majority of the statement, while Other Income and Drawing (the amount you paid yourself from the profits) are added on later.

Net Income = Operating Income + (Other Income - Drawing)

The income statement is computed in a series of steps, which I describe in this section. The order of the statement features is very specific and laid out according to standard accounting procedures.

This is the picture of your **Net Profit** or **Loss** during the year:

Gross Sales
    Less: Sales Returns + Sales Discounts = Net Sales
    Inventory Jan 1 +
    Purchases – Purchase Returns and Discounts
      = Cost of Goods For Sale
    Less: Inventory Dec 31 = Cost of Goods Sold.

    Net Profit on Sales = Gross Sales – Cost of Goods Sold

You then subtract the total expenses of your operations from this number, as follows:

Total Operating Expenses:
Rental Expense
Selling Supplies Expense
Office Supplies Expense
Insurance Expense
Postage and Shipping Expense
Payroll Tax Expense
Sales Tax Expense
Depreciation Expense
Amortisation Expense
Miscellaneous Expense

Net Profit on Sales - Total Operating Expenses
= Net Operating Income

Here is where you account for the addition of income from other sources besides Sales, which can include cash grants you received to complete your project.

Net Operating Income =
(Other Income* - Drawing** + Interest Income) + Net Income

*Other income can also include grants and loans you received for your project. You do not include 1099 Misc income like *net royalties* from your selling partners. These are reported on page 1 of your IRS 1040 and are considered separate from your regular business income.
**Drawing refers to the amount you pay yourself during the course of your business since you are self-employed. When you file your 1040 you must pay the same percentage (15%) of Social Security tax for yourself that you file and pay for your employees. If you are employed elsewhere, your drawing amount will increase your gross income but your 1040 Schedule C will offset the difference for Adjusted Gross Income.

You combine the totals of all these on your *Net Income Statement* at the end of the year:

Net Income Statement Dec 31:
Gross Sales - Cost of Goods Sold =
Gross Profit on Sales - Operating Expenses =

Net Operating Income
+ (Other Income – Drawing) + Interest Income = Net Income

This statement is a summary of your financial condition at any time of the year, and you can calculate this as often as you want. But you need the expanded or detail report to help you report your income from sales on IRS 1040, Schedule C.

The Balance Sheet is the picture of your business's financial condition at the end of the year. It shows the totals of all your accounts adjusted by the business activity per account. This is where the statement:

Capital = Assets – Liabilities

comes into play. But before you can see it you need to learn about the *Balance Worksheet*. It is a summary of all your acounts placed on one sheet. It is usually kept on a separate spreadsheet where you make your adjustments and closing entries at the end of the year.

Many people do not use closing entries but carry over the old balances in the asset accounts into the next year, but however you decide to do it you must make sure that your accounts balance. The worksheet shows that you have integrated your merchandise purchases into inventory and removed inventory which had sold or was disposed of, numbers in operating accounts were moved into the net income statement, and so on.

Note that in all cases the columns must balance; that is, show equal totals, except for net income. In this way you verify whether the balances of all your accounts for the year tally correctly. If any column does not balance it is likely because you left something out or overstated something, which is why the journals and ledgers are so important. This information also helps you to fill out your financial statements. Your year-end balance sheet will look something like this:

Balance Sheet at Dec 31
Assets
Cash
Accounts Receivables
Inventories
Selling Supplies
Office Supplies

Office Furniture – Accumulated Depreciation
Equipment – Accumulated Depreciation
Computer – Accumulated Depreciation
Prepaid Rent
Prepaid Lease
Leasehold Improvements
Amortisation – Accumulated Amortisation
Other Business Assets
 = **Total Assets**

Liabilities and Capital:
Accounts Payable
Interest Payable
Taxes (Income and Sales Tax) Payable
= **Total Liabilities**

Capital
Capital at 12/31
Net Income
Drawing
Other Income
= **Total Capital**

Total Assets = Total Liabilities + Total Capital

You see that the statement is in balance and that this is the actual value of your net worth. You could summarize the capital computation even further by preparing a statement that looks like this:

Statement of Capital Dec 31
Net Income
 + Other Income - Drawing = Net Increase in Capital

Capital at January 1 + Net Increase in Capital = Capital at Dec. 31

Then when you prepare your balance sheet you take the total of your liabilities and compare them with the summary of capital. But in all cases, the total amounts must balance with each other in your business. These two statements are essential for use in your 1040

Schedule C, which helps you to determine your taxable income for the year.

Taxes And Permits, Forms And Deductions

You cannot avoid payment of certain taxes in order to continue to operate your business. During the course of a given business period, you are leaving some kind of paper trail wherever you go, and the governments of your city, county, state and the country are mindful of this. As I discussed before, you must look up the requirements for your particular situation. But when it comes down to various basic needs, I will discuss them here.

Whenever you engage in a business where you deal with people in person and on a day to day basis, you may owe **business tax** to the city where you do business. You pay a fee, and the business then issues a permit to you in order to operate legally. You are then expected to track your business income and deductions as they relate your base of operations.

If you are itinerant, sell out of the back of your truck, or sell your work at various book fairs, your business activities inside the city may not have to be counted. Your state sales permit may excempt you from payment of the business tax.

You can also obtain a city sales permit for the day you plan to sell if you are only an occasional seller, but only if you intend to sell for more than 10 days in any year. The number of days need not be consecutive, and some cities begin to ask for taxes if you sell for more than 5 days in the year. You must consult with your city permit department for more specific information.

The county of your home operations may also charge you to register your **fictitious business name** and they will require you to post the registration on your own in your local newspaper. This is not really enforced, and thousands of business names go unregistered because of the ephemeral nature of their activities. Yard sales do not need ficticious business names.

The county will give you a long time to renew, and the registration may be necessary only if you think someone else is likely to use the same name. If you change the name often, or go out of business in a year or two, it may be necessary for you to declare that the business is closed or that the name has changed. But again, that part of it is entirely up to you and it depends on the county in which you intend to do business.

As long as you continue to actively do business and you have financial activity, the business name is covered by the state sales permit. If your state charges some kind of **sales tax**, you must obtain a tax permit in order to report and pay the tax after the end of the year. If you operate on a fiscal year schedule, this means you must file a **sales tax return** containing the activities of the total calendar year, which includes the sales tax owed across two fiscal years (like the last half of the first and the first half of the second), beginning January 1 and ending December 31.

If you own your own store and/or carry a lease on the property, you may be required to pay a **property tax**, which is a lien on the assessed value of the real estate or the actual physical value of the store. It is similar to the property value of a residential home and treated slightly differently. You may also deduct the *business portion* of the property tax on your home if you use it to conduct your business.

Your state's own requirements may be different, but in California, the **business portion** of your *taxable income* may have to be adjusted by the amount of local taxes paid, or is used to offset your personal income for **state income tax**. If you have employees, you may have to adjust by the amount of unemployment taxes owed to the state. In all cases, your Adjusted Gross Income is often used to determine the amount you owe to your state. You may not owe any taxes at all if your AGI falls below the state's standard deduction amount. If you have a *loss* for the year, you do not owe any tax.

By far the inevitable consequence of doing business is that you must report the income and expenses on your **federal income tax** return. The profit or loss from your full or part time business is reported as net income, and may be used to offset earned income from other types of taxable activity.

In order to arrive at this critical number, you must fill in certain forms which reflect the support for it. It is not enough to throw a number onto the Form 1040 and expect the IRS to accept it without justification of how you arrived at it. Here are some of the requirements you must follow to compute your net income or loss for tax purposes, and I will add the most recent developments from the last tax year as well as new rules instituted.

1040 Schedule C: Profit or Loss From Business

This is the form where you plug in all the values I showed you for reporting your operating income and expenses. Note that some of the expenses you took are not permissable for tax purposes. The form comes in 5 parts: Income, Expenses, Cost of Goods Sold, Auto Expenses, and Other Expenses. If you had business expenses of $5,000 or less, use the cash method of accounting, did not have any inventory, and did not have a net loss during the year, you may be able to file *Schedule C-EZ* instead. You must have had no employees and no home expenses to qualify.

Income. Here you report your Gross Receipts (cash) or Gross Sales (accrual), your returns and allowances including discounts, your Cost of Goods Sold and your Gross Profit. If you are entitled to a state exemption or credit against sales or receive other income as part of your sales activity, you also report it here to arrive at *Gross Income*.

Business Expenses. These are listed in detail on *irs.gov* as **Publication 535** and includes an extensive list. You can use the information to keep accounts of your regular activities. These expenses are totaled and then deducted on IRS 1040 Schedule C . But you are not finished. At the end of this section you can also take expenses related to the use of your home for your business to arrive at *Net Profit or Loss*.

Cost of Goods Sold. Here is where you report any *Production* and *Selling Supplies* used during the transaction and how you arrived at the total of the cost, indirect and direct labor costs, overhead (extra costs associated with the product, like packaging).

If you take a portion of the sales to pay yourself, you report the amount in **Drawing**, which is listed in *Other Expenses*. In the book publishing business, however, your 1099 net royalties are listed on the *Other Income* (line 21) line on the 1040 itself.

Other Costs includes the value of materials discarded in the making of your product. You want to make sure that the loss of your materials inventory is included as you consume them. Discarded materials is expensed as part of the Cost of Goods Sold category. This is used to offset the *Ending Inventory* you computed for the end of the year.

Information on Your Business Vehicle. Here is where you compute the amount of gas or diesel fuel you consumed in the operation of your car or truck if you use it for business at any time. It is essential that you record your odometer readings for this purpose at the beginning of your business trip and at the end. You subtract the business miles from your total odometer reading at the end of the year to arrive at your business mileage deduction. It is a pain, and if it's too hard to keep track of you can take the standard mileage deduction instead, which is enumerated in Publication 535. This deduction is divided and tracked according to averaging data, and can be taken in place of exact figures. It amounts to a fraction of a dollar per mile.

But if you spend most of your time traveling from place to place to conduct business the added bonus of shaving off the right amount of mileage expense from your operating income will prove beneficial to your overall business health. You keep receipts and write what they were for just as you do for all your travel expenses. The expense also covers incidental auto expenses such as oil, transmission and brake fluids, incidental repair items like replacement light bulbs, and others. It can also cover minor repairs if the breakage could be associated with the use of your vehicle during the business trip.

Other Expenses. These include all the other expenses not mentioned in the other three sections like computer time at your local printer, discarded display equipment which is disposable like price placards, signs, and so on; research costs like library fees; rentals of display space which are of a semipermament nature; amortisation expenses as relates to startup costs and intellectual property, and so on.

1040 Schedule SE – Self-Employment Tax The fact is that when you are a sole proprietor and the single employee in your business you must account for your regular income taxes just as you would for your employees if you had them. When you compute the payroll tax for them you withhold half of the 15% of Social Security tax you owe from their wages and pay the other half out of your operating margin. But when you are self-employed you must pay the whole amount for yourself.

Note that the Self-Employment Tax is in lieu of Social Security Tax. The only consideration you are given is that you will pay out **15% of the _net profit_** from your Schedule C *if it is more than $400 and less than $125,000*. Of course you pay nothing for a net loss and you can even omit this schedule if you had less than $400 in net profit. This includes 1099 net income from royalties earned.

File it anyway, even if it is zero, because it will minimize your risk of an audit to determine if you owe the tax in the first place. **When in doubt, file**. It does no harm to you to cover yourself for all these situations. Your investment in the business is considered to be *at risk* for any and all taxes owed so you must be prepared to put all your cards on the table when asked.

These are the basic steps to help you reduce your tax liability for both your business and your personal income. If you have many sources for personal income, you can take a business loss as an offset for **Adjusted Gross Income**. Follow the instructions on your 1040 form to help you list the adjustments in the order they go in, and you might find that you owe less tax automatically.

The Basic Concepts of Economics

Here is where I point out some other considerations about publishing and marketing your book that you may find useful. In order for you to make long term plans which are based on your current selling model, you must know how to look at the numbers in terms of *economy of scale*.

Again, your physical records are maintained as a balance of economic factors, so your general business health is dependent on the number of factors which are of economic worth to you. You have no doubt heard financial analysts speak of concepts like supply and demand, equilibrium, costs and price tipping points, the break even point, opportunity costs, and so on. If you have never dealt with these concepts before it is vitally important that you learn what they are and what they mean to your business.

Demand and Supply. The price of your book depends heavily on the demand for it. As the price of your book goes up, the demand for it will go down. As a book author or publisher, you have an opportunity to sell your book based on the price alone, but your costs will go up as the demand for it goes up. You must always examine your retail price to compare it with your costs or you will end up with a loss on sales every year.

You have seen what happened to the price of gas in the United States because of trading speculation in the stock market. No matter how much supply was made available, the artificially inflated price changed the buying public's behavior, and as a result demand went down. Soon afterward, the price of gas went down again because the market could not sustain such a high price and because people made conscious choice not to buy at that price.

It was not helpful to know that part of the price of gas included taxes designed to fund the maintenance of roads and highways. As far as the public is concerned, if they cannot afford gas at that price they will not buy it. *Period*.

As of this writing the amount of gas being consumed has not changed, and there are other problems with the supply chain which also drive the price up. Production curtailments, natural disasters and war can often limit the supply and make it difficult to trade at a lower price. Now, the supply of oil at the mining level and issues of global trade are also affecting the price, and may be something suppliers may have no control over. However, that is changing even now as the United States has opted to begin domestic production of oil and natural gas, so it is becoming a supplier of these goods and can control the price across the board.

Similarly, if you have a product which cannot meet the price expectations of your customers it is in your interest to lower the price in order to limit the loss of demand.

Supply and demand are also affected by **price and demand**. A book's worth on the marketplace is governed by a number of factors, like genre, topic, author notoriety or celebrity, price, and availability. Just because you have a book available for sale does not mean it will generate the same interest in the marketplace as another. So, a book is not really the same as oil or gas.

It is now considered an extraneous or *luxury* commodity, so demand may not be a good indicator of how well it will sell if all other conditions of the marketplace are met.

Also, the economy may not support the publication of the book, or the readers' interest may be directed elsewhere. It may have nothing whatever to do with the intrinsic worth of the book itself, and does not reflect on your hard work and dedication. This becomes even more difficult when your book may target a niche market.

Those who have risen rapidly on the book lists are simply lucky, and may descend again into obscurity when interest wanes. You should not let perception govern your drive to be successful. One book is not the same as another.

Equilibrium. This is how you can see at a glance how well you are doing in your business. Ideally, you want your *gross profit* to be in balance with your costs, and you compute your *break even point* by charting the changes in sales and costs over the year.

You are in *equilibrium* when your **net sales equal your total costs**, and you *break even* when you can pay your costs without incurring a loss. This is beneficial to determine if your costs could stand some paring down. Your break even point should always break at a higher level than the junction between your net sales and your costs of operation. This is where increasing your *profit margin* is critical to attaining equilibrium and keeping it.

Many banks look at the functioning equilibrium of your business to determine the risk to them if they lend to you. As I discussed before, if your *liabilities* exceed the amount of your *assets* and *capital*, you are not in very good business health, and banks will be less willing to lend to you.

In fact, no business I know of has ever actually balanced at perfect equilibrium. But the most successful ones are able to post enormous profits inspite of whatever costs they incur because they employ good business planning to achieve their success.

Costs and Pricing. I have already discussed the actual values in the section **How To Price And Sell Your Book** but here you want to compare the *quality* of costs against the price you set. If after a while you realize that the sales of your book is going down due to outside factors, you look to your unit costs to see why. Maybe the cost to print has gone up, or the commission fees have gone up, or there is a decline in demand for your particular genre, or even that the cover design could stand a change and is lowering your expectations for the success of the book.

To drive sales you can hold a discount sale, or you can lower the *list price* for your book permanently. But ultimately your book may have to be updated to recapture the public's interest. This means you will have to spend more money to make the book more desirable.

You want to keep the list price the same or less, or you will hit what is called the *tipping point* for the price of the book, which occurs when your readers will not buy the book at the price you set. If you have already taken all the other factors into account this can be catastrophic. But you then have to treat the updated book like a new book, and you absorb the *opportunity costs* of selling your old book into the cost of the new book as the *difference* in actual costs between the new book and the old book.

This is where the value of a revised edition comes into play. You can use this edition to renew the public's interest in your story. Some authors have been able to achieve this by stating that the revision is an update of the old edition and gaining repeat customers that way. They also attract new customers who want the most current information possible. It all depends on the subject matter of the book and how popular the genre is.

Cookbooks, for example, are always popular because each author is presenting a new way to prepare a meal differently. If one can present a new recipe for quiche Lorraine using a brand new ingredient, that is what makes the book that much more valuable to lovers of food or cooking.

You can also change the cover and title. This may generate interest among many new customers you were not able to reach before. The cost of generating this new cover design becomes the opportunity cost for the continuation of your sales. The long term value of the investment you make to drive sales becomes actualized when your sales increase. I have continued to look for ways to make my fiction saleable, while I need do nothing for my nonfiction. There is nothing wrong with experimenting to see what combination will work to make all your books money making products.

A Word About Customer Service

As you establish and extend your business, whether with books or some other product; how you project your personal appearance and behavior to others is of paramount importance.

In this century, we hear about surly behavior, rudeness, lack of proberty or communication among clerks who are hired to answer questions and service the needs of customers in large department stores and chain retail stores. At the turn of the 19th century, sales companies made it abundantly clear to their clerks and outside salesmen that they must always behave toward the customers as knowledgable, helpful, polite and concerned. This appears to have lapsed in recent years, after the turn of the 20th.

A example of this is with the clothier Abercrombie & Fitch, which caused damage to its business by stressing the "sexiness" of its product line. While there is nothing wrong with this tactic at a basic advertising level, A&F began to promote the concept with a bit more aggression than it should have.

Photos of underage boys and girls wearing adult clothing which made them look more mature than they were outraged the general public, or so it would appear. Vocal groups against the exploitation of children fought back by demanding that A&F take the ads down, or modify them so they were not quite so provocative. A&F fought back by calling the groups disparaging names on the public forum.

In response the groups called for a steady boycott. Apparently, this was very effective, and A&F backed down facing angry shareholders.

Now, Lululemon Athletica is having a similar problem when it publicly announced that its line of yoga wear would not accommodate overweight or fully formed women. The backlash drove its profits down below what is acceptable for a company which has been around forever.

These situations illustrate a large company's loss of vision with respect to the customers entering their stores, and those customers can now do more than simply complain to the store managers. They can now orchestrate a huge outcry on the public forums by means of the internet, which is rapidly overtaking the shopping choices for people all over the world.

As these companies face a loss of reputation as well as harsh criticism for their business decisions, they have been humbled by the mantra: *the customer is always right*.

As you deal with any customer or supplier, you must project the most professional and friendly attitude possible, because you are ultimately responsible for the success or failure of your business. I have experienced many situations myself; in person and online, that told me the clerk or representative did not care about me as a customer. The fact is that anyone you must convince to buy your book is expecting to be treated like a *king or queen*. Otherwise you will not have a sale that day.

Let me cite another example of what I am talking about. Some years ago, I was riding home from work on the bus. I did this rather than drive because I was trying to save money by a) not using too much gas, and b) not paying for a parking space. It was a hot summer, and the bus was almost full.

A young man got on the bus toting a tray full of sunglasses. I should say he elbowed his way on, because he did not wait for anyone to get off first. Then he marched up and down the aisle declaring that he had these "cool" sunglasses for sale. By his attitude and body language, his whole presentation spoke of, *"buy them because I have them for sale,"* not *"buy them because they are great sunglasses."*

He sat down next to me and tried to sell me a pair even though I was already wearing a pair myself. It was all, "buy them from me anyway."

I said, "no."

"Why not?"

"Because I already own a pair of sunglasses, and I am wearing them now. I don't need another pair."

He proceeded to curse at me. I told him he just lost a sale and to take a hike. And as he looked around at the other passengers, it was clear they were not going to buy them from him, either, because they were all glaring at him. He grumbled, got up and got off at the next stop, cursing all the way.

I have no doubt that he did not make a single cent from his business because he broke the cardinal rule of sales: **you do *not* try to *force* anyone to buy your product**. You do not speak rudely to them, because what you say may lose the customer's trust and his business. Many young people do not understand this rule, and then are surprised when the manager hands them an exit package at the end of the day.

How To Relieve Stress and Enjoy Your Success

At the end of the day you must have a warm glow in your heart for the fruits of your labor. After all, writing and publishing a book should be fun, not just hard work. If you do not feel that way there is something wrong with the way you approach your work day. Here are some solutions which will make you feel better no matter what occupation you pursue:

Sleep. You remember that I said that making time for friends, family and outside activities should be balanced with your writing or production time. I said that *sleep* should also be an important part of your routine.

Your brain is a machine just like any other piece of equipment you use in your business. It needs down time, maintenance and repairs. Every part of your lifestyle should be geared toward maintaining its health. Sleep is an integral part of that and the quality of sleep is essential, not just the number of hours you devote to it. If you do not have a good night's sleep you will work yourself to exhaustion and the quality of your book and its production will go down.

Sleep is based on your personal *circadian rhythm*, which is governed by the time of day you were born. Your whole life energy comes in cycles. If you are a day person you wake up early and go to sleep early. If you are a night person you wake up late and go to sleep late. If you try to work against either one you are fighting an uphill battle every day, which can lead to exhaustion no matter if you worked that day or not.

Your sleep cycle is also based on whether you keep a day job to pay the bills, the kinds of foods you eat and when, and also if you use alcohol, drugs or tobacco to help you cope. You should look at your own habits and lifestyle to determine if you should change the routine in favor of a better sleep cycle.

Eating food too close to bed time, for example, can keep you from falling asleep. Try to eat your last meal closer to sunset and you will find that you will fall asleep faster. Above all, shorten or cut out those activities which waste the amount of sleep time you have available to you. Some rely on Melatonin to regulate their sleep cycles. I use it, but my sleep cycle depends on darkness and quiet. I generally turn off the television set no later than 1:00 am, because if I don't, I will stay up all night.

There will be times when you cannot get away, or a family matter is too important to ignore. These can eat into your sleep time, too, but it is important that you include them. If you find yourself too wired up to sleep because of things that happened that day, let yourself stay awake and fall asleep when it happens.

The effort to sleep is just as tiring as the lack of sleep itself. If you can avoid using a sleeping pill do so. A cup of hot chocolate or warm milk instead can often help.

Eat better foods less often. Your body depends on a whole range of different foods to function well, and your diet can affect your writing ability. The human race has evolved from a tiny, skinny primate into a giant. Our natural body shape is slim and light, not large and heavy. Mankind was born to chase after his food and it is only in the last two centuries that we have stopped. Now, most of what we eat comes from the local supermarket or the local eatery. Our athletes and celebrities must train to retain their physical attributes, and are considered the standard for physical beauty.

The admonition that one should eat 3 meals a day to maintain good health has long been criticized as a path to bad health because it encourages people to eat more than they need to. This view has been challenged by medical experts, so it is no longer so important to your good health to eat 3 meals. Eat when you are actually hungry, not because it is there. Your caloric intake governs how well you function. Too much food is worse than far less.

It is also a sad fact that a majority of people in the United States are overweight or obese, relying on a fast and easy diet which causes chemical imbalances in the brain and body. These changes can lead to a variety of conditions and diseases such as high blood pressure, heart disease, pulmonary diseases, diabetes, and even allergic reactions to foods such as peanuts and chicken. Some of it is due to the genetic makeup of the person, and may have nothing to do with lifestyle. Some are addicted to food and use it as a coping mechanism for the other stressors which ail them.

It is not just the quality of the food but the amount which is at issue. The time-honored *eat when you are hungry* plan has resurged in the dietary community as the best way to approach the proper diet. It stresses moderation to make it effective. You can adjust your daily intake to two meals per day, or sometimes just one, with small snacks in between. Depending on your genetic makeup you can avoid getting many of the diseases mentioned above through moderation alone. The fact is that many people can get away with one large meal a day supported with a small series of snacks, like fruit and vegetables.

While I like junk food like chips and snacks, candy, cookies, and the like, I know that I cannot rely on these foods alone for my good health. But there are many people who have grown so self-indulgent that junk food is what they live on, instead of a good mix of meats, fruits, nuts, and vegetables. They reach for that can of sugary soda instead of a glass of water. They also binge on certain foods to excess. Their bodies become ever more dependent on an excess of sugars, salts and carbohydrates to function, while they are unaware that they are killing themselves slowly with these habits.

Many use food to maintain the comforts of living without realizing that they are only making themselves more miserable. The junk food habit includes a skewed self-image which some use to justify their need for the food which is doing them harm. They also enjoy their condition, which is a side effect of the addiction itself, and will fight to preserve their lifestyle as much as possible.

Their bodies reflect their diet in the form of adult acne, red cheeks, shortness of breath, elevated heart rate, excess sweating, flatulence and odd body odor, spare tires, excess cellulite and fat pockets where they do not belong. I know women who are skinny everywhere but their thighs, where the fat has concentrated. They are carrying as much as 50 lbs. in each thigh, which places even more stress on their spines.

It may be natural that human children must eat as much food as is necessary in order to grow. But they are also prone to overindulge due to a variety of emotional issues, such as household conflicts, lack of self-esteem, and other stressors. There is now an epidemic of obesity among children in the United States because of the ease and amount of food they can obtain, while not addressing the causes of their stress.

If you want to avoid becoming a victim of your love of food you need to examine your own self-image and determine if you can make a change for the better. As your body's health improves you will feel better about yourself, and your writing will improve. As a consequence your emotional state will improve, so that you can write better, and feel good about yourself and your work. Call it a feel-good snowball. Stay proud of yourself.

Avoid alcohol, recreational drugs and tobacco. I am serious. If you cultivate a habit of writing while drunk or stoned you will also become addicted to the process for tweaking your creativity, instead of using your natural wit. It is no longer true that a drunk writer makes for an interesting personality or character. Sometimes a drunk is just a bad writer.

The same is true for drugs. You can save your body and mind from the effects of addiction; not to mention the amount of money you save from not buying the drugs at street value. It can be downright embarassing if you get caught, and will do more damage to your reputation as an author than anything else. If you find that you have to write using mind altering drugs you are dishonoring yourself and your talent.

Tobacco is now the number one cause of cancer, emphysema, cardiopulmonary conditions and advanced aging, leading to an early death. Tobacco is also highly addictive, and will become the controller of your daily routine in short order. The cost of a pack of cigarettes these days can represent a drain on your finances, too. If you stop smoking you will save as much as $5,000 per year and thousands more for medical treatments.

It is vital that you value your emotional well being as well as your body, so avoid these energy vampires if at all possible. Your writing will improve radically if you keep a supply of small snacks, water, and a period of nap time by your side instead. Respect yourself and you will gain more respect for you and your work from others.

Exercise your body as well as your mind. Physical movement is essential to keep you from dying at your keyboard. You can take as little as ten minutes each day to extend your body's health, and you do not even have to leave your office or bedroom. You would be surprised how many story ideas you get while exercising.

Stretch yourself out, use objects for resistence weights, play with your dog or cat, climb up and down stairs, clean your office, dance, have sex. Take some time off and go for a short walk around the block, go to the gym, use your floor cycle, or practice yoga. I use yoga extensively myself, as well as calisthenics and isometrics in place. Get your heart rate going to feed those little grey cells inside your skull. Your physical health will add greatly to your emotional health.

The use of ergonomic chairs has been widely recommended but they can be expensive. If you do not have one, sit so that your back is straight and your legs have plenty of room to move. Adjust the height of your monitor so that you can see straight ahead instead of at a downward angle.

If you work on a laptop be sure that the angle of the screen does not force you to look down too much. Take some time out to let your head fall back slowly to work out that kink in your neck, and repeat your exercises if you begin to feel stiff.

Remember: writing a book is not a race. There is no rush to finish it. If you set a deadline to finish it, shame on you.

Make some time for yourself. A certain amount of solitude is necessary to avoid something I call *sensory overload.* It is your brain telling you that it is tired and everything is too much to handle at that moment. We all spend a good portion of our day dealing with outside stimuli which constantly intrude on our lives and demand our attention, such as television noises, gardeners with leaf blowers, the neighbor's dog barking, people arguing, loud music played nearby, etc..

Sensory overload is there, often whether we are aware of it or not. Some people can handle the stress by tuning noises out. Others cannot, and need quiet in order to work. But often there is no place one can go to get that.

When civilization was more primitive, people were bombarded by the sounds of crickets and frogs, birds, the sound of the sea, the sound of the wind, but grew used to these noises and learned to tune them out. But with the advances we take for granted, unnatural sounds have taken over to intrude on our solitude. Some are so loud they can cause damage to eardrums and optic nerves.

If sounds become too loud, or the light too bright, or you get a headache, excuse yourself and walk away, turn off the noisemakers in the house and just sit, or engage in some other activity which does not demand too much of your attention. Allow your brain some time to reboot and adjust.

Be sure to make a schedule which includes a day of **ME time**. Go to the beach, or hike in the mountains, or sleep. Change your environment in order to eliminate the amount of stimuli pounding on your nerves. In this way you will preserve your sanity and the good quality of your work.

There was a time when I had to leave the city altogether and work in a hotel room because construction noises next door kept distracting me. If you do things like this, you can shorten the time you have to work to finish your project, and less disruptive than yelling at your family or neighbors.

Make your work space work for you. The use of *feng shui*, or the balance of elements, has a proven benefit to the output of your work. The amount of floor space you use, the arrangement of your office furniture, their placement with respect to doors and windows, the overall color scheme and even the color of your walls can have a profound effect on your psychological well being and your productivity. If you feel like the color yellow drives you crazy, paint your walls blue or some other color you like.

Many authors like lots of space, others feel good in what amounts to a broom closet, but it is vitally important that you make a place of comfort so that you can focus on your work.

The presence of clutter can also dictate how much work you are likely to do in that room, and may even distract your and impede your productivity. If you feel hemmed in by the presence of clutter, clean it out. I have found that by cleaning I can think about my project and come up with new ideas.

If you like music played in the background, make it a part of your routine. The use of music has been proven to be a great work aid, because it reorders the centers of the brain which are responsible for your creativity. Certain kinds of sounds also stimulate the brain to produce the serotonin and endorphin levels necessary for a creative experience, which in turn makes you more productive.

If you are not sure about this, I recommend you look this up on *Wikipedia* and articles available in issues of *Science*. The use of music has long been used in office environments and work places to create an atmosphere of calm and productive discipline for decades. That elevator music is there for a reason.

Aromatherapy is also useful. Burn a stick of incense, or a fragrant candle, or keep live flowers in the room, or wear your favorite perfume.

In other words, it is up to you to make all the necessary adjustments which will help you to focus on your work.

Maintain your self esteem. If you are serious about your craft, do not let your friends or family, coworkers or strangers, try to deter you or steer you away. If they tell you that writing or whatever else you do as your chosen profession is a waste of time, ignore them. How many times have you heard someone tell you to get a *real* job? What is a real job, anyway? It is only an activity which earns money.

Be proud of what you do, because your work defines who you are. Live your life with your head held high because you are achieving your goals through hard work and study. But if others try to take an active part in stopping you, confront them with the idea that it's your life and you will decide what to do with it.

If they are your parents, then you are not receiving the proper support from them based on *their* expectations of what *their* lives are supposed to be like, and they are placing them squarely on your shoulders. If you have this kind of problem seek counseling from your teacher or professor, or even your clergyman. Sometimes just having feedback from a supporter outside of your family will steer you back on the right course. Remember that you are *you*, not somebody else. Your life choices are yours alone.

A few words about writer's block. If you are starting a project the hardest way is to sit in front of your keyboard and stare at a blank screen. Do not do that. The problem with writer's block is that it is a self perpetuating procrastination engine. The more you worry that you have it, the more the worry will stop you from going forward. You are like a piece of metal which has been newly minted. The more you hammer away at it, the stiffer and more brittle it becomes. Learn to recognize the root causes of writer's block and take steps to abolish it. Of course you can write. So what's stopping you?

Here are some ideas to help you break the perception.

1. **Writing a book is not a race.** There is no deadline for finishing it except when you have commited to one, and that is an automatic no-no. Take as much time as you need to write your book, and do not allow anyone to pressure you to finish it before you are ready. You are better off waiting until you finish the book *before* you offer it to your publisher, or when you are close enough to finishing it that you know you will make the date.

2. **Take a notepad, pick up your pencil or pen and write whatever comes into your head about your project.** Doodle, scribble, play with words, think about what you want to say and write it down to use as an anchor for your focus. Write down bits and pieces of dialogue; design a character. Write a short outline or a scenario. You would be surprised what you come up with. If your head is just not that into it at the moment, work on something else. The point I am making here is that it will still be there when you get back to it.

I get frequent and amazing ideas when I am watching television and a concept materializes from a line of dialogue, an image, or from listening to someone talk about something else entirely. It is my brain which forms the idea, and I must do something to incorporate it into my current work.

3. **The best and most natural writing comes when you are not setting any limits to your creativity**. Take as long as you need to start, and take all the steps necessary to ensure the free flow of ideas and words. Do not worry about what comes out. Many people use *stream of consciousness* to craft the first draft of a novel by simply typing whatever comes into their heads without structure, then going back and editing later. The use of this technique will free you from the perception that you cannot write. Remember that your editing aids, the 4 books I listed at the beginning of this book, are there for a reason. Your use of words is as much a craft as if you were carving a piece of wood. Experiment. Try it from a different angle. Read articles about a particular topic to gain a better understanding.

4. **If you find that you have run out of ideas at the end of the day, stop and do something else, then come back to it later**. Some people begin several projects at once so that there is no end to their creative output. As they lose focus on one project they work on something else until the creative logjam is broken loose.

5. **If your personal life is so full of problems that they cause your focus to break, it is a good idea to attend to them first**. You have to know your priorities as well as your limitations. There is plenty of time to take up writing again, and unless it has the ability to grow legs your book will be waiting for you like a faithful friend when you return.

In Conclusion

This book was designed to answer the most common questions about publishing and marketing a book or any other product you care to produce. I have only scratched the surface. There are a great many other questions you are bound to ask when you approach the publication of a book or the creation of your product.

I chose to narrow the choice of topics to just the basics and I have omitted product design concepts and other information which relate to the creation of other products. If I did include them, the book would easily balloon to 500 pages or more. As you use the information you will be able to become an expert at solving whatever problems come your way. On the internet there are also thousands of service providers, information and culture mavens, as well as thousands of other authors like myself who have chosen self-publishing to break out of the dungeon the large publishing houses use to confine us.

I have also included lists of URLs and contacts for each kind of service to help you on your way, but you can find many more on Google, Yahoo, or whichever search engine you use. As you learn which kinds of options you have you will be able to know where to look.

Thank you for purchasing this book, and I hope it has pointed you in the right direction. Good luck in your new career.

Bibliography

The following are books and magazines selected especially for your continued education in the world of book publishing and includes some design considerations for book covers, layouts and the like. They include some reference books for the history of books and printing which I have added here:

Ptolemy, fl. 2nd cent. **Cosmographia**. Roma, 1478. With an introd. by R.A. Skelton. Amsterdam, Theatrum Orbis Terrarum, 1966.

Celtic illuminative art in the gospel books of Durrow, Lindisfarne, and Kells, by the Rev. Stanford F. H. Robinson, M. A. Dublin, Hodges, Figgis, & co., limited, 1908.

The book of Kells : a selection of pages reproduced with an introduction and notes / by G.O. Simms. New ed. Dublin : The Dolmen Press & The Library of Trinity College, 1968.

The Canterbury tales / Geoffrey Chaucer ; a verse translation with an introduction and notes by David Wright. Oxford [Oxfordshire] ; New York : Oxford University Press, 1985.

Durer, Albrecht, 1471-1528. **Woodcuts of Albrect Durer**, by T. D. Barlow. London, Penguin Books [1948]

Stillwell, Margaret Bingham, 1887- **The beginning of the world of books**, 1450 to 1470; a chronological survey of the texts chosen for printing during the first twenty years of the printing art, with a synopsis of the Gütenberg documents. New York, Bibliographical Society of America, 1972.

Observations Concerning the Increase of Mankind, Peopling of Countries, etc., by Franklin William Goddard (US patriot & publisher)

"**Introduction**". Autobiography of Benjamin Franklin. Macmillan's pocket English and American classics. New York: February 1, 2011.

Benjamin Franklin. "**Part three**". The Autobiography of Benjamin Franklin.

Benjamin Franklin. "**The Pennsylvania Gazette**". FranklinPapers.org, October 23, 1729

Philip L. Richardson (February 8, 1980) "**Benjamin Franklin and Timothy Folger's first printed chart of the Gulf Stream**," Science, vol. 207, no. 4431.

Fleming, Candace. **Ben Franklin's Almanac: Being a True Account of the Good Gentleman's Life**. Atheneum/Anne Schwart, 2003, 128 pages, ISBN 978-0-689-83549-0.

Anderson, Douglas. **The Radical Enlightenments of Benjamin Franklin** (1997) - fresh look at the intellectual roots of Franklin

Chaplin, Joyce. **The First Scientific American: Benjamin Franklin and the Pursuit of Genius.** (2007)

Autobiography, Poor Richard, & Later Writings (J.A. Leo Lemay, ed.) (Library of America, 1987 one-volume, 2005 two-volume) ISBN 978-1-88301153-6

"**Poor Richard's Almanack**." Peter Pauper Press; November 1983. ISBN 0-88088-918-7

WIKIPEDIA –The open resource (*www.wikipedia.com*)

THE WRITER'S MARKET an annual book edited and published by Writer's Digest Books and published by F & W Publications, Cincinnati, OH.

ARTIST'S & GRAPHIC DESIGNER'S MARKET another annual book edited and published by Writer's Digest Books and published by F & W Publications, Cincinnati, OH.

ACCOUNTING Barron's Business Review Books
© Barron's Educational Series; New York. Any edition will do.

An overview of all the bookkeeping principles I outlined in this book and also some concepts I left out due to their lack of relevence to the tracking of records in your small business. But it is an excellent textbook if you want to learn about accounting in the larger business world.

The Writer's Digest and **The Artist's Digest**
The American Artist (magazine)
Communication Arts (magazine)
end

CPSIA information can be obtained
at www.ICGtesting.com
Printed in the USA
BVHW042000031219
565535BV00010B/143/P

9 781732 531284